HOUSE OF GIN

THIS BOOK IS DEDICATED
TO MY FAVOURITE HUMAN
BEING, MY HUSBAND, ALAN.

THE MAN WHO GETS
ME, PUTS UP WITH ME
AND COMPLEMENTS ME.

GIN IN HAND, LET'S
CONTINUE TO DREAM
THE SAME DREAMS.

ANDY CLARKE

OVER 40 COCKTAILS TO SHAKE,
MUDDLE AND STIR AT HOME

Hardie Grant

BOOKS

CONTENTS

ROOM
1

ENTER THE HOUSE OF GIN

THE HALL
5

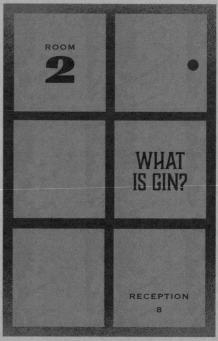

ROOM
2

WHAT IS GIN?

RECEPTION
8

ROOM
5

HOUSE CLASSICS

THE CONSERVATORY
42

ROOM
6

HOUSE SPECIALS

THE LOUNGE
74

ABOUT THE AUTHOR
138

ACKNOWLEDGEMENTS
139

INDEX
140

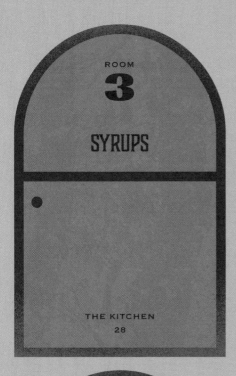

ROOM

3

SYRUPS

THE KITCHEN
28

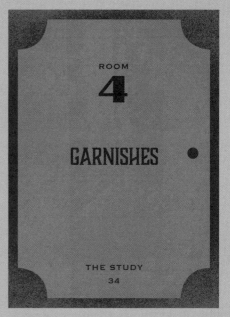

ROOM

4

GARNISHES

THE STUDY
34

ROOM

7

DRINKS
FOR EASY
ENTERTAINING

THE DINING ROOM
106

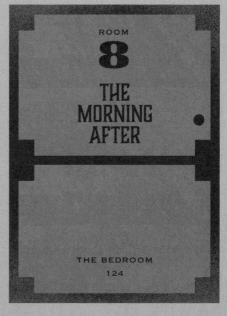

ROOM

8

THE
MORNING
AFTER

THE BEDROOM
124

ENTER THE HOUSE OF GIN

Welcome to the House of Gin.

Come in, get comfy and let's fix a drink together.

Pull up a bar stool and enjoy thumbing through the pages of this guide to some of the best gin cocktails in the world.

There is so much variety in gin and the cocktail possibilities are seemingly endless. I've really enjoyed re-discovering some of the classics, so much so that I've put 15 of my favourites in here. I also love getting creative when tasting gin and imagining how the flavour profile might work in new concoctions, so there are dozens of new cocktails here for you to try.

I want to empower you to understand and enjoy gin in a way that you've never done before. In this book, there are explanations of gins and mixers, cocktail-making tips, guides to cocktail kit and glassware, ideas for garnishes and ice that will take your cocktail making to the next level plus, of course, fabulous cocktails for any occasion.

This book is for people who might be short on time but big on gin cocktails, so I've tried to make sure that the recipes aren't complicated or time-consuming. (After all that's what cocktail bars are for, right?) I'm keen to make sure that you feel that you are being ably supported in your pursuit of the perfect cocktail. To ensure that this book is easy to use, you not only get step-by-step instructions, I'll also fill you in on a bit of the history, the best types of gin to use, the dominant flavours and the best time to enjoy (and I've resisted the temptation say 'any time' every time!). There are icons to show you at a glance the best gin style to choose and the seasons it suits best.

I've planned something for everyone, but please, when making these recipes, feel free to make them your own. Add more, add less, scribble your own twists and suggestions on the recipes and enjoy playing around with the flavours.

Whether you're chief cocktail maker, chief cocktail sipper or simply experimenting with gin or even with 'low & no' gin substitutes, you are all very welcome to the House of Gin.

Now go dust off your bottles and fix a cocktail to put a smile on the faces of you and your guests.

A BRIEF HISTORY OF GIN

When sipping gin, you don't always think of the rich history that has brought this unique and beguiling drink to your lips. Generations of people have developed thoughts, ideas and processes that have allowed gin to evolve into the drink that we know today. But where did it start?

Although historically London has always been associated with gin production, it is thought that its origins actually hail from just over the English Channel in mainland Europe. Since the Middle Ages, people have believed in the possible medicinal benefits and healing power of juniper berries, while the alcoholic juniper-based drink, often known as 'genever' (the name coming from the Dutch word for juniper) dates back to the 13th century. In the 16th century, we believe a gin-style drink was distilled with juniper berries for medical purposes, and by the 17th century, it was well known. It was at that time that the expression 'Dutch courage' was first coined, with reference to the Dutch soldiers who drank genever during conflicts to give them courage. I can certainly sympathize with the notion that gin consumption can make you feel invincible! It seems not unlikely that the English soldiers who fought alongside the Dutch wondered where their comrades' bravery was coming from! And so a version of the drink came to England. It was from here that the anglicized name 'gin' was developed.

Roll on the early 18th century, when gin became extremely popular in England, particularly in London, possibly because of high taxes for beer and wine as well as the increase of alcohol import taxes. It seemed that anybody could make gin, and they did. Whilst it was legal, it meant that it wasn't regulated and there are reports of gin often being flavoured with liquids such as turpentine and even sulphuric acid.

This period is known as the 'Gin Craze' and subsequently caused social problems, including crime, illness and death, which were famously depicted in William Hogarth's 1751 engraving entitled 'Gin Lane', the ultimate depiction of the results of the excessive consumption of gin. In the same year, an Act of the Parliament known as the Gin Act of 1751 was enacted in an attempt to prohibit gin distillers from selling gin to unlicensed merchants and consumers, therefore reducing the consumption of gin and hopefully alleviating the problems that had existed up to that point.

While the negative connotations of gin such as expressions like 'gin joint', 'gin soaked' and 'mothers' ruin' live on, now more in a jovial sense, the popularity of gin continued and the story of gin became a bit more positive! The creation of styles of gin like 'London Dry', the development of pot-still techniques to distil gin and the popularity of the gin and tonic gave gin a more sophisticated reputation going forward into the 19th century.

In the 20th century, gin remained a popular drink that the world couldn't get enough of, even when people weren't supposed to be enjoying it. 'Bathtub gin' refers to the illegal batches made behind closed doors during the American Prohibition of 1920–33, when the manufacture, distribution and sale of alcohol were made illegal. It was basically a home-steeped gin! Cheap alcohol was mixed with water and botanicals to produce a, shall we say, 'rustic' alcoholic drink. Gin cocktails also became incredibly popular in the early 20th century. Iconic recipes were being created across the world and *The Savoy Cocktail Book* by Harry Craddock was published in 1930. Featuring a huge number of gin cocktails, this legendary book is a classic and has inspired many drinks writers today – including me!

The early 21st century saw a resurgence in gin popularity, especially amongst young people of drinking age who might previously have seen gin as a drink for their parents' generation. Whilst there was a great deal of respect for standard gin types such as London Dry, Plymouth, Old Tom and the newly coined Navy Strength gin, the next generation of gin was rising. Popularity grew through the emergence of small-batch distilleries all over the world. With a new generation of gin-makers came new ideas untrammelled by convention, which excited the palates of Generation X and Millennials. While the global hospitality industry took a major blow with the Coronavirus lockdown of 2020, the world embraced their home bars and artisan distilleries used the time to develop new ideas and sell their gin to people desperate to re-create cocktail bar standard drinks in their home.

Now, it's hard to move for gin bottles in many households, including mine. And I'm excited for the future of gin.

WHAT IS GIN?

If you're reading this book, you're probably as gin-obsessed as I am but how much do we really know about gin? We know how to drink it, but I know I'm guilty of never really analysing it or giving credit to the talented people who make the good stuff. So here I've collected together everything you need to know about gin – and never dared to ask!

WHAT IS GIN?

Gin is essentially a clear alcoholic distilled spirit usually made from a base ingredient of grains or potatoes. In order to be called gin, it must be flavoured with juniper berries, which provide the light, piney note. The further layers of flavour that we love in gin – and the reason there are so many different types – is that so many other botanicals, such as citrus peels, spices, barks and herbs, can be added in an infinite variation so the possibilities for gin distillers are endless.

Gin is a drink that is usually around 40% alcohol by volume (ABV) and must be over 37.5%. Gin liqueurs are usually around half that volume as they are a mixture of gin and other ingredients such as fruit or sugar. Navy strength gins are 57% or above, but more on that story later.

HOW IS GIN MADE?

The alcohol is created from the base ingredient – usually wheat or barley but sometimes potatoes or other grains – which is fermented for 1–2 weeks, producing alcohol (ethanol).

This ethanol is then distilled – in some cases, once or twice, or even many times.

Distillation is the process whereby a liquid (in this case alcohol) is purified by heating it up, turning the liquid to vapour and then collecting it as it recondenses into a liquid. This gets rid of impurities and creates a purer product.

At various points during the distillation process, juniper berries and other botanicals are added, which is what creates the flavour.

The liquid formed as a result of distillation is not the same throughout the process:

♦ The first 35% can be volatile or toxic and are often known as 'heads'.

♦ The next 30% is known as the 'hearts', which are considered the best liquid to use.

♦ The last 35%, known as the 'tails', although impure, are often kept and redistilled for another batch.

Once the distiller is happy with the distilled pure alcohol, it is then mixed with deionised water to achieve the desired ABV. (Deionised water enables the botanical oils to remain in suspension, making it a clear spirit instead of cloudy.) The completed gin is then sampled and bottled.

There are different ways of distilling; here are the main methods in a nutshell.

POT-STILL STEEPING

Alcohol and botanicals are combined in a metal container called a pot still, which is put over a heat. The botanicals steep in the heated base spirit.

VAPOUR INFUSION

This method involves a still with a basket above it. The botanicals are placed in the basket and when heated, the alcohol vapour rises into the botanicals. Once the vapour turns back into a liquid, it will be infused with the botanicals.

VACUUM DISTILLATION

A low-pressure vacuum is used, which reduces the alcohol's boiling point. It is sometimes thought that by avoiding heat, the flavour and character of botanicals are retained more effectively than using other methods.

TYPES OF GIN

Gin is not just gin! There are so many different types to get our heads and our lips around. As a gin drinker, I was guilty for many years of not really knowing as much as I should. Here I would love to help empower you to more informed gin drinking. If you know what you're putting in your glass, you'll make better cocktails.

LONDON DRY

Probably the first type of gin that we think of when gin is on our minds, London Dry is often the first gin that starts a person off on their gin journey. It is usually crisp, striking and juniper-led. Essentially, it's a straightforward gin, which is great with tonic and to add to a cocktail.

The term 'dry' in relation to gin refers to the unsweet characteristics that juniper and other botanicals give the aroma and flavour, and it was coined in the 18th century. The term 'London' refers to the fact that this style of gin was most commonly produced in London, England. However, contrary to what you might think, gins that are 'London Dry' do not have to be produced in London. It is not a PGI (protected geographical indication) reference. London Dry gin actually refers to a type of gin-production process – which can be made anywhere.

♦ Gordon's, Tanqueray, Beefeater and Greenalls are names that are recognized all over the world as being London Dry gins.

♦ And whilst there are so many producers making London Dry gin, one of my favourites is 6 O'Clock Gin, a small producer from my home town of Thornbury, near Bristol in the West of England.

NEW WESTERN DRY GIN

Whilst London Dry is a much loved and specific type of gin, there are many dry gins around that aren't London Dry and therefore will not be labelled as such. 'London Dry' is not an indication of quality. Other dry gins that aren't London Dry can be delicious and well worth trying.

This recent movement is known collectively as 'new western dry gin' and it encompasses what we know as craft gin, boutique gin, artisan gin and small batch gin that have become increasingly popular over recent years. Whilst juniper is prominent, new western dry gins are often the result of a lot of experimentation with emphasis on other botanicals.

♦ Hendricks and Aviation are big names in this movement, and there are many other new western drys being made all over the world.

♦ Some of my favourite small batch distilleries include Madame Jennifer, Cygnet, Thunderflower, Boathouse, Echlinville and Anholt.

PLYMOUTH

A unique gin as it is the only gin with PGI status, it is named after the English city of Plymouth in the county of Devon, where it has been made since the late 18th century. It was first produced at the Black Friars Distillery and is traditionally a dash sweeter than London Dry gin. Plymouth gin places greater emphasis on 'root' botanicals, like angelica and orris root, with only subtle hints of juniper, resulting in a slightly fruitier taste.

Plymouth Gin is a not only a style of gin but also a brand of gin that has been distilled on the same premises on the Barbican in Plymouth since 1793. Its worldwide fame was helped by the British Royal Navy, which took it on ships all over the world.

OLD TOM

A slightly sweeter gin than both London Dry and Plymouth styles, Old Tom became popular in the 18th century when some producers added honey or sugar to disguise inferior-quality gin. It is thought that the name came from the wooden plaques shaped like a tom cat that were mounted on the external walls of some pubs serving the gin in 18th-century England.

Over the years, London Dry became a more popular gin but recently Old Tom has enjoyed a bit of a resurgence because of its versatility in cocktails. Some of the Old Tom gins I've tasted recently have a warming hint as well as a sweeter edge, which can be delightful in a cocktail.

- ◆ Well-known brands of Old Tom include Hayman's & Jensen's who both also make London Dry.

- ◆ Other smaller great Old Tom gins include Gorilla Spirits, G&H Spirits and Mother's Ruin 1751 which makes Commander Fox.

NAVY STRENGTH

The term refers to gin that is higher in alcohol than the majority of gins. For a gin to be classed as Navy Strength it needs to 57% or above.

The origins of Navy Strength gin go back to the 18th century when the British Navy took gin with them on voyages. The gin was stored next to gunpowder. It is thought that if the gin got into the gunpowder, the gunpowder would still explode if the gin was of high alcohol content. Whilst stories of Navy Strength rum were in the history books, the term 'Navy Strength' became popular in the 1990s and is how we know stronger gins today.

My advice when using Navy Strength gin is, if you fancy a strong G&T or you are making a longer-drinking cocktail, feel free to use it. But if you are making a strong gin cocktail like a martini or a potent smaller cocktail (of which there are many) it's best not to use a gin with 57% or more alcohol!

- ◆ A good example of a Navy Strength Gin is Scilly Spirit Distillery's Atlantic Strength Island Gin.

GENEVER

Sometimes written as Geneva, Jenever or Jeneva and also known as Hollands or Dutch gin, Genever originated in the Netherlands. It is made using a botanical-infused spirit (basically a gin) and malt wine, which as a bit like an unaged whisky or whiskey. As you can imagine, it has a malty flavour and can feel richer in viscosity in the mouth.

BARREL AGED

Increasingly, small distilleries are experimenting with ageing their gins. Small-batch, barrel-aged gin is becoming popular amongst gin-lovers and involves leaving gin in wooden casks or barrels, in much the same way as whisky or whiskey is aged. Ageing gives gin oaky, spiced notes and richness of texture – a bit like the gin version of a barrel-aged wine! Whatever was previously stored in the barrel will affect the flavour and character of the gin. The colour of aged gins will often be more golden rather than clear like non-aged gins.

If using aged gin in cocktails, be aware that it will impart a richer flavour than non-aged gins so use it only in cocktails that have other warming flavours.

♦ Salcombe Distilling Co. make a cask-aged gin called Victuallers' Special Edition Finisterre, which is smooth and delicious.

SMOKED GIN

It's not something you see a lot of, but it is a thing. It has a rich, pronounced flavour profile thanks to the liquid being introduced to smoke. A smoked gin can be satisfying to sip neat at room temperature or over ice, but be cautious using smoked gin in a cocktail as it will significantly change the overall taste.

♦ Fishers make a smoked gin worth trying.

♦ Gin Bothy also make a lovely smoked gin.

PINK

It is thought that pink gin was created by those serving in the Royal Navy by adding Angostura bitters to Plymouth gin. The bitters were first used as a treatment for sea sickness from 1824 by a doctor called Dr Johann Siegert and the addition of gin was considered to make the bitters more palatable. This later became a popular cocktail later in the 19th century.

Pink gin has since taken many forms and you can still buy it today. Always pink in colour, the flavour profile of pink gin varies between manufacturers. Some have bitter notes as a nod to the bittersweet origins of the drink and others are a bit more like candy floss or cotton candy!

I advise caution when buying and using pink gin in your cocktails as they can differ greatly. If you're keen on finding a pink gin that works for you, why not try making your own using Angostura bitters and your favourite gin (preferably a Plymouth or Old Tom) with a dash of sweetness to balance the bitters.

♦ Isle of Wight Distillery's Mermaid Pink Gin is exceptional.

SPICED, FLORAL, ZEST OR CITRUS

The gin explosion of the early 2000s saw many gin distillers experimenting with different flavours. Often these gins are marketed as spiced, floral or zest (otherwise called citrus) gins, which whilst they don't intend to give one dominant flavour, go in a different direction to that of a traditional London Dry or Old Tom. The flavours of these types of gin often lend themselves to being used in specific cocktails because of the addition of certain botanicals.

Spiced gins are popular with people looking for a hint of warmth and often contain spices like cinnamon, ginger, cardamom, mace, fennel seeds, peppercorns and cumin.

Gins with a floral leaning are sometimes also labelled as 'garden' gin and they will often contain petals and oils from flowers such as rose, elderflower, hibiscus, jasmine, lavender, chamomile and violet as well as various garden herbs.

When I'm talking about zest or citrus gins, I mean gins that have a leaning towards citrus rather than outright flavoured gins. These will be citrus-forward and contain flavours from the outer zest of various citrus fruits, but won't specifically taste of one particular fruit.

- Opihr is a spiced gin that sums up this style.

- Griffith's Brothers Distillery's spiced gin is also great.

- Drumshanbo Gunpowder Irish Gin, whilst not labelled as a spiced gin, does have oriental botanicals giving a warm comforting taste.

- Otterbeck Distillery make a spiced and a garden gin worth trying under their brand 'Cotton Gin'.

- Brewdog's Lonewolf gin has a zesty citrus kick as does Feckin Unbelievable Irish Gin.

COASTAL

Some gins are considered to be coastal gins. These tend to be gins that contain botanicals that grow around the coastlines of seas and oceans. Sea herbs, sea plants and seaweed are often used to give a fresh, sometimes saline, flavour profile. Some have also been infused with sea shells such as oysters. Whilst often having a freshwater character to them, they don't tend to be savoury. They will still have a balanced flavour with juniper balancing out the coastal botanicals and minerality from the shells.

- Menai Oyster Gin from the Llanfairpwll Distillery is a beautiful sip.

- Bullards Coastal Gin is worth a sip if you're looking for this flavour profile.

FRUIT FLAVOURED

This is quite a broad category. Let's face it, there are a lot of flavoured gins on the market (of varying quality). The idea that you can add a dominant flavour to a traditional gin base has opened the floodgates to the idea that 'anything goes' as far as gin production is concerned. Juniper and traditional botanicals take much more of a supporting role in flavoured gin. More conventional examples are flavours like citrus (orange, lemon and pink grapefruit are all popular) as well as an array of berry flavours. Rhubarb is also a really sought-after flavour in gin. Pink peppercorn is an obvious variation as spices are often used anyway, it's just a case of adding more into the process.

There are too many flavoured gins around the world to name here, but here are my tips when buying flavoured gins or using them in cocktails:

♦ Always go for flavoured gins with natural ingredients that will provide realistic flavours rather than artificial flavourings, which can actually taste synthetic. If you're like me, you won't want your gin to taste like somebody's dropped a packet of boiled sweets in it!

♦ When choosing to add a flavoured gin into a cocktail, always consider the other ingredients and the overall flavour profile of the cocktail before adding. Not all flavoured gins will work.

♦ If you're unsure whether to use a flavoured gin in a cocktail, make a mini cocktail with less liquid volume (but the same proportions) as the written cocktail so that you're not wasting ingredients.

It's important not to be afraid of experimentation with flavoured gin – that's how new cocktails are formed. If you don't like what you've made, just don't make it again!

♦ Some of my favourite fruit flavoured gins come for Rugby Distillery.

♦ Malfy also make some very pleasing citrus fruit gins.

♦ Warner's Distillery have a range of innovative flavoured gin variations.

♦ Check out Sloemotion Distillery's fruit gins – they're great.

SLOE OR DAMSON

I've given sloe and damson gin their own section rather than grouping them with fruit-flavoured gin. This is because they are classed as gin liqueurs, due to the fact that they are slightly sweeter and contain less alcohol than other gins.

Sloe are the small berries of the blackthorn tree. They are in the same family as plums and cherries and are grown in a variety of regions around the world. Sloe gin became popular in the UK in the 17th century after a series of Parliamentary Acts that turned common land into farmsteads and properties. Blackthorn trees were commonly used as a natural divide to break up land, which brought sloe berries to the nation! It was soon discovered that their fruity yet tart flavour imparted beautifully when steeped in gin and sugar.

Often considered a great Christmas gift because you can make sloe gin at harvest time in autumn, it is more of a gin liqueur really, as there is sugar involved and the alcohol content is around 20–30% ABV. So, if you have been given some and don't know what to do with it, get your shakers and out and try using it for cocktails.

On a similar note, damsons are small sour plums and are often used to flavour gin. Damson gin is also a delicious alternative and can be used in the same cocktails that you'd use sloe gin.

I have included specific sloe gin cocktails in the book, but you could use damson gin instead. As for the majority of cocktails that are not designed for sloe or damson gin, you could substitute clear gin with sloe or damson, but only in some of the fruitier cocktails (particularly those where the flavour is citrus-forward). You would just need to use less sweetener.

♦ Hogg Norton make a fruity and beautifully balanced sloe gin (as well as a fabulous sour cherry gin liqueur).

♦ The Wiltshire Liqueur Company also make a rather lovely sloe gin.

♦ Chilton Liqueurs and Foxdenton Estate both make exquisite damson gin as well as a range of other delicious gin liqueurs worth trying.

GIN LIQUEURS

Be aware of the difference between a flavoured gin and a gin liqueur. A flavoured gin will have approximately the same alcohol content as a conventional gin (around 40%) and whilst it will have a distinct flavour, it won't be overly sweet. A gin liqueur will contain significantly lower alcohol (usually around 20% and sometimes up towards 30%), have sugar or an alternative sweetener added and will be more syrup-like. You would not drink a gin liqueur in the same way or quantity that you would a gin, whether with a mixer, or in a cocktail.

As well as the producers above, other great gin liqueurs are available from:

♦ The Lakes Distillery
♦ The Oxton Liqueur Company

TOO MANY GINS, NOT ENOUGH TIME

Please note that the flavour and quality of gins on offer changes all the time, especially when they are from small batch producers, so use your judgement and find your favourites!

I'm also aware that there will be many gins that I haven't had a chance to taste, but that doesn't mean they're not lovely ... I think the expression is: too many gins, not enough time.

Whilst through my work I am experienced in a lot of British and Irish gin, I am aware there are great brands all over the world that are relatively easy to get hold of – including Xoriguer from Menorca, Kyrö from Finland, Gin Mare from Spain and Roku from Japan.

But wherever you are in the world, I encourage you to support local.

THE BEST MIXERS

This section comes with a warning: not all mixers are the same! While your choice of gin is crucial to the success of your cocktail, the other ingredients must also be top quality. Sometimes it's nice to change things up a bit, so here's my guide to different mixers you can try with your gin.

TONIC WATER

The clink of the ice as it hits the glass, the splash of the gin as it cascades over the ice, the fizz of effervescence as the tonic mixes with the gin. We all love a G&T, right? It really is the perfect way to start any celebration. It's a drink that is refreshing and transcends seasons – it's perfect at any time of year.

Tonic water is essentially a carbonated soft drink which contains quinine (from the bark of cinchona trees). Citric acid and sugar or other sweeteners are often added to achieve a specific flavour. Some are quite bitter, some are more tart, and others can be a tad sweet, so it's important to select one that works with your choice of gin.

The name itself was patented in 1858 and was made by Erasmus Bond who owned Pitt & Co. in Islington, North London, but its history goes back before then when it was originally used as a prophylactic against malaria. Once it was discovered in South America that quinine could help the battle against malaria, it was then added to sparkling water and sugar in order to make it more palatable to taste by British army officers stationed in India.

Today, there are countless brands of tonic.

♦ Schweppes is a well-known brand that makes a classic gin and tonic when mixed with a London Dry.

♦ Other brands I use at home come from companies like Fever Tree, the Artisan Drinks Company, Franklin & Sons and Double Dutch.

I'm aware that there are loads of producers the world over, so try different brands and find a tonic water that works for you.

Yes, tonic water is a great mixer with gin. (I also love a virgin tonic water with a big squeeze of lime on the rare occasion that I'm avoiding alcohol!) But there are so many flavoured tonics out there these days. As with flavoured gin, it's impossible to list every single one. It is worth noting that they vary widely in quality due to the ingredients used to flavour them. If you are going to sip a flavoured tonic, make sure it's one that uses natural ingredients. Also, try a dash with your gin to make sure that it is a nice combination. If trying as flavoured tonic with a flavoured gin, be cautious. Two distinct flavours may go nicely together, but they may jar – they're not always a match made in heaven.

CUCUMBER
TONIC WATER

One of my favourite G&T variations is cucumber tonic water. The light and refreshing flavour of cucumber can go beautifully with a gin with the right flavour profile.

♦ Fever Tree make a lovely one. And it pairs nicely with a gin like Hendricks.

PINK GRAPEFRUIT SODA

Sodas are just as nice to have with gin. Ok, they don't have the gentle bitter notes of a tonic, but straight soda can feel incredibly refreshing with gin and a squeeze of your favourite citrus fruit. There are also a lot of flavoured sodas out there. Whilst I encourage you to try some, as with flavoured gins, I'd avoid ones that give you that boiled-sweet effect!

You'll realize as you read this book that I love citrus, particularly pink grapefruit. And the bittersweet tones of a pink grapefruit soda are delicious with a citrussy gin.

♦ Franklin & Sons make my favourite pink grapefruit soda; it's refreshing, zesty and incredibly mouthwatering.

GINGER BEER
AND GINGER ALE

Ginger beer can be a really fun mixer to have with gin. When it was created in 18th-century England, it was an alcoholic drink made from fermenting ginger, sugar and water. These days, whilst it's still called a 'beer', most commercial versions are non-alcoholic or very low in alcohol. There are some delicious, fiery versions out there, which are made with real root ginger.

While similar to ginger beer, ginger ale is a little lighter in flavour. It's not as intense and often not as spicy. It is a gentler ginger mixer to have with your gin.

A spiced or aged gin can work really well with these two effervescent gingery drinks as the warming notes from the spiced botanicals integrates nicely with barrel-aged gin.

COLA

It's not the first mixer you reach for when you think of gin, but in a similar way to ginger beer and ginger ale, there are notes in the flavour profile that actually do work with spiced or aged gin.

Colas are carbonated and tend to contain kola nut, vanilla, cinnamon and citrus oils. If, like me you're not that fussed about widely available commercial colas, try some of the smaller artisan varieties that you might be able to get your hands on. I find that you get more layers of flavour from some artisan colas.

♦ My choice is the Artisan Drinks Co. barrel-aged cola, and the cola made by Hartridges.

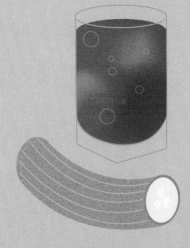

KOMBUCHA

Kombucha is an effervescent, fermented, tea-based drink. It is made by fermenting using a symbiotic culture of bacteria and yeast (known as a SCOBY) and often called a 'mother'. It is commonly thought to have originated in China around 220BCE, before becoming popular in Russia and then Europe. Kombucha has increased in popularity over recent years with producers popping up all over the world making a variety of what we presume to be authentic versions. It seems that every year there are more producers and it is increasing in popularity with consumers.

Kombucha tends to have a crisp citrus flavour and can be exciting and revitalizing. It usually has an alcohol content of 0.5% which puts it in the 'low and no' category of drinks. I like pure versions that are not flavoured as they allow zesty citrus, mellow tea and biting green apple flavours to excite the palate.

As with other mixers, there are many flavoured versions of kombucha, some being a little too sweet for my palate (although this is tempered when balanced with gin). Ginger, however is a winner when added to kombucha.

Kombucha can make a great mixer for gin. Experiment and see what works for you. Like any drink, kombucha recipes differ from batch to batch and there are so many companies making it now that it's hard to keep on top of the state of play. Kombuchas that I rate include:

♦ Craft Tea Brew Co.'s range of kombucha

♦ The Healthy Guy Company (Original and Ginger Gem)

♦ Life Kombucha (Jasmine Green Tea and Apple, Lemon, Ginger)

♦ LA Brewery (Citrus Hops, Blush and English Rose)

SPARKLING TEA

In the same vein as kombucha, sparkling tea is a popular alternative to dry sparkling wine. The gentle herbaceous and floral flavours in sparkling tea are often beautifully delicate and work nicely with the gentle bubbles within the drink. Sparkling tea is also a nice mixer with gin as it brings out the botanicals.

Some of my favourite sparkling teas are:

♦ The Real Drinks Co. (Royal Flush / Peony Blush / Dry Dragon)

♦ Jing (Jasmine Pearls)

JUICE

Gin and juice is a simple yet wonderful combo. When I was younger, I used to hear my parents' generation talking about 'gin and orange'. OJ is a brilliant mixer for gin, but it actually turned out that some people in their circles would mix gin with orange cordial! I can see how adding some sparkling water might make this more palatable for me, but anyhow, I digress! What I am saying is that freshly squeezed fruit juice can be a great mixer for gin, especially if a dash of sparkling water is added. If you have juices such as orange, apple, pineapple or tropical mix or a cranberry juice drink in the fridge, give them a whirl with gin. I think you'll be pleasantly surprised.

COCKTAIL TIPS

Gin cocktails are fun, celebratory and exciting so the cocktail-making process should be too. It really doesn't have to be hard. When ordering a cocktail in a bar, the experience can be quite theatrical and lengthy, which can put people off doing it at home. But don't be discouraged. You can do it! Here are some tips and things to remember when making gin cocktails that will help you feel like you are winning.

BE ORGANIZED / BE IMPROMPTU

Yes, it's great to be organized. You can make syrups, juice fruits, make ice and even fix entire cocktails ahead of time, so that you can get your gin fix quickly when required. But if you just get the urge to have an impromptu martini, or a last-minute gin fizz, you don't have to worry that your cocktails are going to take ages to make. Often at home if I fancy a cocktail before dinner, I forego the garnish and I don't worry too much about the glassware. Yes, it's nice to make a cocktail as beautiful as they are in your favourite cocktail bar, but don't stress if it looks a bit 'rustic'.

TASTE

The first rule when it comes to making a cocktail for yourself or friends and family is to remember that everybody's palate is different. I have designed these gin cocktails using my own sense of flavour. We all have different palates, there is no right or wrong. If you want to add more of certain ingredients into your cocktail to make it work for you – just do it.

INGREDIENTS

I have designed these cocktails using the gin and other ingredients that I am able to buy where I live. The spirits, mixers, juices and fruits you use may be different from the ones I have used; there are many brands across the globe. Even local items of the same fruit variety vary in flavour. Just make sure you taste before you serve. After all, you wouldn't serve a meal you cooked without checking it first!

PARTS

As well as specific quantities, each recipe specifies the proportions of the ingredients; it's all about the ratio of each ingredient to the others to create the perfect balance of flavour and texture. Meaning, as long as you know how much ingredient you have in relation to the other ingredients, you'll always have a great cocktail.

♦ 1 part + 1 part + 1 part means that you have three ingredients of equal measure.

♦ 2 parts + 1 part + 1 part means you have equal measures of two of the ingredients and twice as much of third.

Glasses differ in size from manufacturer to manufacturer. I've seen martini glasses that are twice the size of mine (but size doesn't matter!) Knowing the proportions also means that it doesn't even matter if you don't know the volume of your drinks measure. I tend to use a jigger – a double-ended measure so you can use it for a 25ml/1½ tbsp and 50ml/1½fl oz capacity – but if you don't have one and don't know how much your shot measure holds, no problem: use a thimble, a measuring spoon, a shot glass, a ramekin or anything you can find really. Be inventive, the lid of a cobbler shaker can be used as a measure and a recipe tester, for instance.

THE FROTH DEBATE:
EGG WHITE, AQUAFABA & THE DRY SHAKE

I love the luxurious feel of a velvety cocktail. To achieve this, egg white is widely used, and more increasingly aquafaba, which is the water from a can of chickpeas (garbanzos). By using a couple of dessertspoons of it in your cocktail shaker, it will give you the same effect. Rather than adding flavour, egg white and aquafaba add a frothy texture. It's easy to think about omitting this in your gin cocktail making, but I urge you to use these frothy helpers if the recipe requires them. They really will make all the difference.

In order to get the best results, it's best to do a 'dry shake', where you shake the ingredients together first without ice. This is because you will get the most foam when the egg white or aquafaba are at room temperature. If they are ice-cold, they will not be able to perform their magic as well. All you need to do is shake the egg white or aquafaba along with the other liquid ingredients in the shaker for 10 seconds before adding the ice. This lets the protein in the egg white or aquafaba begin to form foam. Then add the ice and shake for at least 20 seconds, which is the amount of time it will take to chill your drink. Feel free to shake it for longer if you like, but you don't want the ice to melt and for it to dilute your cocktail.

LOW & NO ALCOHOL GIN

Year on year, the quality and quantity of non-alcoholic gin substitutes gets better. If you're not up for the hard stuff, you can replace alcoholic gin with 'low & no' alternatives. There are so many good examples out there now, being made by reputable producers all over the world. The hit of the cocktail when you taste it will be different, so I suggest, if you're an alcohol drinker, that you find your favourite by sipping it neat in order to achieve the flavour profile that is the most similar to your favourite alcoholic gin. Whether or not you drink alcohol, avoid using 'low & no' gins that are too sweet.

If you feel that your cocktail needs more zing, use a dash of lemon or lime juice to bring the flavour profile up to where it needs to be.

♦ Pearsons Botanicals, Lyre's, Sipsmith and Salcombe Distilling Co. make their own versions which are worth a try.

MUDDLING

I love to muddle! It's a great way to release flavours and aromas from herbs and fruit and it allows you to get the most out of your ingredients. Here's how to muddle like a pro:

♦ Drop your herb and/or cut fruit into your cocktail shaker, jug or glass.

♦ Find a muddler. You can buy a muddler or you can use any clean, long implement! (Something like a wooden spoon or a rolling pin with a rounded end.)

♦ Add the gin and slowly and firmly press the muddler into your receptacle and gently twist it in one direction in order to crush your herbs and/or fruit.

HOW MUCH ICE?

Here's a simple rule – the more ice you put in your shaker, jug or glass, the colder your cocktail will be. It might sound silly that I'm saying that, but there is a misconception that the more ice you put in, the more it will water down the drink. This isn't true. It's quite the opposite. Putting only a couple of cubes of ice in your shaker or jug drink means the ice warms up quicker than if there is lots of ice in it. This results in your drink being diluted faster. Fill your receptacle with ice and your cocktail will stay cooler for longer.

For a variety of different ice ideas, head to pages 38–40.

SIP HAPPY

Gin cocktail drinking is fun and celebratory. Cocktails are a symbol of good times. By entering my house of gin, I want you to be happy and to enjoy some cocktails that put a smile on your face. I want to encourage people to 'sip happy'. Don't drink to numb the pain, to forget or to get depressed ... drink to celebrate life and enjoy yourself. Let's focus on the positives. After all, there's a lot to smile about.

YOUR COCKTAIL KIT

As a proud cocktail maker, I love having a collection of cocktail equipment. Like wearing old faithful clothes or snuggling under your favourite blanket, I have shakers, jiggers and glassware that I adore and that make me smile when I use them. But one thing is really important: don't feel that you have to splash out on specialist equipment in order to enjoy cocktails at home. Yes, you need something to make and serve your cocktails in, but if you need to get creative, don't worry if you don't have the exact equipment. Get ready for your guide to essential equipment and some alternatives that will help you enjoy your gin cocktail experience.

CHOPPING BOARD

Using a specific chopping board for fruit and veg is essential – I don't want you cutting your garnishes on a board that's had raw meat or fish on it! A chopping board is also a great surface for when you're juicing, measuring liquids and making cocktails. It saves you getting your surfaces sticky. It's easier to wash your chopping board in the sink than mopping-up the spillages on your counter tops.

COCKTAIL SHAKERS

There's something about using a cocktail shaker that makes the whole cocktail-fixing experience feel special. There are two main types of shaker and both have their benefits.

♦ **THE COBBLER SHAKER** is the sexy-looking shaker that I love to use. My eyes light up when I see one. There's something so classic about the lines of this three-piece shaker which was invented in the 19th century when a removable cap was added to the classic two-piece French shaker. It's really easy to use and perfect for a couple of low-volume cocktails. I love that you can use the lid as a little taster to see if the cocktail is up to scratch before serving.

♦ **THE BOSTON SHAKER** is a two-piece shaker consisting of a large metal base cup and a glass or metal top cup that wedges in once you're ready to shake. The advantage of this shaker is that you can fit more in it than you can in a cobbler as it has greater volume. But the downside is that you sometimes have to bash the shaker to open it. If you use one, just don't damage your surfaces!

♦ **NO SHAKER? NO PROBLEM!** It's always better to shake cocktails if you are looking for an ice-cold serve and if you are using egg white or aquafaba for texture. So, if you need to shake but you don't have a shaker, use a jam jar or a water bottle that you have washed thoroughly. They will have exactly the same effect as the shaker. You can also stir many cocktails. Other than the frothy ones, it's really up to you whether you'd like to have your gin shaken or stirred.

JIGGER

When making cocktails you'll need some form of implement to measure liquid. I spoke briefly about my jigger (or shot measure as I used to call it) when talking about parts earlier in the book. They come in all shapes and sizes, some with measures written on the side, some less descriptive. The one I find easiest to use is a classic jigger you see in many bars – one side measures 25ml/1½tbsp and the other measures 50ml/1½fl oz. But if you don't have a specific jigger, you can use a measuring jug or anything that holds liquid. I find a shot glass, a thimble or a ramekin can work just as well. As long as you work in parts (page 19) you will still get the same fab gin cocktails – just make sure you have enough volume in your jug or shaker.

JUGS & PITCHERS

Jugs are really helpful for both pre-measuring liquids as well as mixing and serving cocktails. Having a few small jugs around is handy for storing juice and other liquid ingredients ahead of cocktail making as well as being the vessel you'll need for stirring a small cocktail for two. Larger jugs or pitchers are perfect for batch cocktails. Having a stylish pitcher to hand (and a plastic one for outside entertaining) is great. But if you haven't got an array of jugs, you can mix and serve from a saucepan or a mixing bowl and a ladle.

JUICER

I'm going to be controversial here – I don't believe you necessarily need to go to town on buying an expensive juicer. As with wine bottle openers, the simplest are often the best. Gin cocktails are traditionally reliant on a good amount of citrus (especially lemon and lime) so it's really important to work out which juicer works for you.

I'm going to be even more controversial now – I love freshly squeezed juice but if you don't have time or you are simply making a lot of cocktails, you can buy pre-squeezed juice – just make sure you're buying quality.

♦ I use Funkin Pure Pour juice pouches which are 1kg/2lb 4oz of pure juice. There is real character to the juice's flavour and it makes a difference to the flavour profile of your cocktail.

MUDDLER

A muddler is a blunt handheld utensil that enables you to crush herbs and fruit in order to release juices and oils. You can buy specialist muddlers that have rounded, blunt ends but if you don't have one, using a rolling pin with a blunt end or a wooden spoon works a treat.

PESTLE AND MORTAR

This famous kitchen pair are your best friends when wanting to crush dried or brittle garnishes into crumb or dust form. They're also handy for muddling herbs and fruit if you aren't able to do it in the shaker. And they look great in your kitchen or home bar.

SEALED BOTTLES & CONTAINERS

Bottles with lids and what I call 'clipable' containers are essential when making sugar syrups (or even a cocktail in advance). Just make sure they are airtight. You don't have to buy specialist containers, as you can rescue suitable bottles or containers before putting them in the recycling.

SHARP KNIFE

Because there's a lot of fruit slicing involved in cocktail making, I suggest you keep your knife as sharp as possible. And a sharp knife when used correctly is much safer knife than a blunt one. When sharp, you put less physical pressure on the knife because the sharp blade is doing all the work for you, especially where thick-peeled citrus fruit is concerned.

STIRRER

Yes, a stirrer is basically a spoon. You can use a dessert or tablespoon when mixing a drink in a small jug, but when stirring batch cocktails, you'll need a long-handled stirrer (known as a bar spoon) to get right to the bottom of the pitcher. There's nothing worse than realizing that the sugar syrup is at the bottom of your jug, when it should be evenly distributed throughout. Specialized bar spoons can look beautiful – they can be metal, glass, have twisted handles, have stylish paddles at the end – but don't go forking

out if you don't need to. You can use a wooden spoon or a spatula – just get right down to the bottom of the jug and lift up to make sure that all the ingredients are blended.

STRAINER

Using what I call a tea strainer (otherwise known as a fine mesh strainer) isn't essential but it can strain your drinks to make them pure, smooth and pip-free! I don't always use a strainer as I quite like my cocktails to have the fruity bits from freshly squeezed juice. If you don't have a specialized strainer, strain your juice through a small strainer or a clean piece of muslin (cheesecloth).

STERILIZING

It is important to sterilize any container that you are going to use to store your syrups or cocktails. To sterilize, I wash containers with antibacterial washing liquid and clean warm water, swill with warm water to remove any suds and then cover the container and lid with boiling water. Discard the water, being careful not to scald your hands, and leave to dry and return to room temperature before filling with ingredients.

The recipes list the equipment you need to make the cocktail so you can have everything to hand, but since you always need a measure of some kind, I've left that out for ease of reading. Some cocktail shakers have a built-in strainer and others don't if you have a cobbler shaker, for example, you won't need the separate strainer. You will also need the equipment to create the garnish, which are listed in the relevant recipes.

GLASSWARE

Glassware can make the occasion of sipping a cocktail really special. There's something exciting about selecting your favourite glass for the occasion. While in this book I suggest which glasses you can use to serve your gin cocktails in, these are only suggestions – you can use whatever you happen to have to hand. Don't let not having the right glassware get in between you and your gin!

If you do want to treat yourself to the right glasses, here's a guide to the glassware I like to use. Oh, and by the way – if you'd like to chill your glasses before serving a cocktail, please do, but personally I don't have time or space to chill mine so I don't expect you to either!

BALLOON

It is thought that the balloon glass originated in the Basque region of northern Spain and dates back to the 1700s. I always think they look like an oversized wine glass, but some gin lovers love them, and they've certainly had a resurgence over the early 21st century with many gin brands creating their own and selling them as gift sets. They definitely grab your attention. My issue is that when full of gin, tonic and ice, they can become quite top-heavy. There's also a tendency to fill them up with too much drink as they are so big. Just remember – deploy the ice to fill the space! You'll appreciate it in the morning!

COUPE

One of the prettiest glasses, the coupe is classy yet cheeky. It is widely believed that this curvaceous glass was created in the 18th century and was inspired by the breast of Marie Antoinette, wife of Louis XVI of France and the last queen to reign before the French Revolution. They are great for small volume, sparkling and still gin cocktails. I love vintage etched versions, and there are often many styles in charity shops, bric-a-brac stores and antique shops. When making a cocktail to be served in a coupe, please be aware that they can vary greatly in size. I have two sets of coupes at home, and one set holds twice as much as the other!

COLLINS

The collins glass is a tall, thin glass with straight sides which is slightly thinner and taller than a highball glass. There's not a huge amount of difference between them but the collins glass looks a little more elegant. They don't tend to hold as much liquid or ice as a highball and because they have a smaller opening, I don't feel that they give a drink the chance to open up as much as if it were in a highball or lowball glass. They are not as easy to get hold of as highball glasses, so if you don't have them, or can't get your hands on any, don't worry, just use a highball.

FLUTE

An elegant glass perfect for gin cocktails containing dry sparkling wine, the long stem and curved lines are inviting and a flute looks even nicer with bubbles inside. Because the flute is narrow, it allows only a small surface area so the drink retains its effervescence. If the glass allows the drink to have a greater surface area, the drink will go flatter faster. I don't know about you, but if I'm honest, I never let a fizzy drink hang around long enough to go flat!

BALLOON

COUPE

COLLINS

FLUTE

HIGHBALL

HURRICANE

LOWBALL

MARTINI

MUG

NICK & NORA

STEMMED WINE

GLASSWARE

HIGHBALL

A tall glass traditionally used for serving gin and tonic, this is the perfect glass for serving long cocktails with a high proportion of mixer. They are great glasses to accommodate a large amount of ice, plus they are perfect for hydrating yourself with water between cocktails. Believe me – if you can down a highball glass of water in between your cocktails, you'll thank me in the morning!

HURRICANE

The shape of this glass says 'party'! It originated in New Orleans, a place that I certainly associate with cocktails and good times, and is named after the hurricane lamp of the same shape. This curvaceous glass lends itself to fun, fruity, cocktails (the type I associate with sunny beaches). But just be aware they can vary greatly in size. My hurricanes are huge (ooh-err) but I know some are so small they'd fit inside mine. If your glasses are big, don't be tempted to make twice the volume of cocktail. Just fill up any excess space with ice or you'll regret it!

LOWBALL, ROCKS OR OLD-FASHIONED

The lowball, as I call it, is also known as a rocks glass or an old-fashioned glass (because of the fact it's perfect for spirits and cocktails like an old-fashioned that are served 'on the rocks' – in other words poured over ice). I know traditionally a highball would be used for a gin and tonic, but this is my choice of G&T glass! I love that you can also use large pieces of ice in them (and they're perfect for my clementine ice cubes, page 39).

MARTINI

The martini glass is a beautiful classic. This stemmed glass with an inverted cone top is an absolute stunner. Its clean lines are a more modern take on the Champagne coupe, which came first, and the slightly more rounded cocktail glass of the 19th century. Some have said the martini glass came about as part of the American Prohibition movement, but it actually had its first formal outing at the 1925 Paris Exhibition and established its popularity throughout the 20th century. I love that the glass allows a cocktail a large surface area so you can take in the fragrance of the drink within. They are great for strong cocktails that you enjoy in small sips.

MUG WITH HANDLE

Sometimes you need a mug with a handle to serve your cocktail. Some cold cocktails traditionally come in them, but they're mainly used when serving hot cocktails. Whilst you can just serve hot cocktails in the same mug or cup you have your tea and coffee in, I think it's nice to use metal (particularly copper) or glass mugs – just make sure they are designed for hot drinks as you don't want them getting damaged or smashing.

NICK & NORA

These cute glasses, originally known as a little martini glass, date back to the 1930s. They became popular in the 1980s and were named Nick & Nora glasses by bartender Dale DeGroff, who was hired to look after the bar at the Rainbow Room restaurant in New York City. He named them after cocktail-loving fictional detectives Nick and Nora Charles who were created by Dashiell Hammett for his 1934 novel *The Thin Man*. You can't find these glasses everywhere, but you can hunt them out in specialist bar and glassware shops. They often come with beautiful etching on too. They are probably my favourite cocktail glass and perfect for small, punchy gin cocktails.

STEMMED WINE

There's something elegant about a stemmed wine glass, and they can make a good vessel for the right cocktail. Larger wine glasses are great for frozen cocktails or those containing wine. They also prove a great alternative to the classic gin balloon glass if you don't have any. Stemmed dessert wine glasses are also elegant. I use them for sweeter or richer cocktails that you sip in small amounts.

SYRUPS

Syrups are an essential part of cocktail making, especially when working with gin. It's important when getting creative with syrup that you complement the botanicals in the gin. These syrup recipes are designed specifically with gin in mind and will allow you to create cocktails with the right level of sweetness and flavour.

As well as making cocktails fun, they're great to add to a gin and tonic or in soda if you fancy changing things up. Because you can make them well ahead of time and store them in the fridge for weeks, they also make it easy for you to be impromptu with your cocktail making.

I use fresh and natural ingredients where possible and I urge you to do the same. However, I understand that it's not always possible to create a syrup for every occasion. There are plenty of pre-made flavoured syrups on the market, so I have a word of advice if you're not making your own: please try to stick to syrups that are made using natural ingredients and are additive free. You really will notice the difference when tasting your cocktails. Synthetic flavours will ruin your creations so keep it natural if you can.

So, before you create your garnishes or fix your cocktails, if you're in the mood to change up your syrups, read on and get your saucepans out!

SIMPLE SUGAR SYRUP

Makes about 250ml/8fl oz

This is a classic that can help you balance out the flavours of your cocktails. If you're not happy with the sweetness level in your drink, a teaspoon or two of simple sugar syrup can be like a magic wand waved over the top.

EQUIPMENT
hob
measuring jug
saucepan
scales
storage container
wooden spoon

PROPORTIONS
2 parts sugar
1 part water

INGREDIENTS
200g/7oz caster (superfine) sugar
100ml/3½fl oz water

1   Put the sugar into a saucepan and pour over the water. Stir and heat gently over a low heat until the sugar has dissolved.

2   Once all the sugar has dissolved and the mixture starts to boil, remove from the heat and leave to cool for at least 10 minutes.

3   Put in an airtight sterilized container and use in your fabulous cocktails. This will last in the fridge for 2–3 weeks.

HONEY SYRUP

Makes about 400ml/14fl oz

This is an easy way to get the scented sweetness of honey into your cocktails. Runny honey is not runny enough to integrate into your cocktails without help. This is a great alternative to simple sugar syrup.

EQUIPMENT
hob
measuring jug
saucepan
storage container
wooden spoon

PROPORTIONS
1 part honey
1 part water

INGREDIENTS
200ml/7fl oz runny honey
200ml/7fl oz water

1   Pour the honey and water into a saucepan and stir gently over a low heat until the honey and water have amalgamated.

2   Once the mixture starts to boil, remove from the heat and leave to cool for at least 10 minutes.

3   Put in an airtight sterilized container and use in your sumptuous cocktails. This will last in the fridge for 2–3 weeks.

PINK GRAPEFRUIT SYRUP

Makes about 450ml/15¾fl oz

I've always loved the joyful bitter-sweet flavour of pink grapefruit. The balance of biting acidity and energetic sweetness is fabulous and I think it's a great addition to citrus-forward gins.

EQUIPMENT
chopping board
citrus juicer
hob
measuring jug
peeler
saucepan with lid
scales
sharp knife
storage container
strainer
wooden spoon

PROPORTIONS
2 parts sugar
1 part water

INGREDIENTS
1 pink grapefruit
150ml/5fl oz water
300g/10oz caster (superfine) sugar

1   Using a peeler, take the zest off the grapefruit, making sure that you don't take off any of the white pith underneath (doing so will make your syrup bitter).

2   Put the zest in a saucepan with the water and sugar. Bring to the boil, then cover and simmer for 10 minutes, stirring occasionally to ensure the syrup doesn't burn. Remove from the heat.

3   Juice the grapefruit and add the juice to the syrup. Stir and pour through a strainer into a sterilized airtight container so that you separate pips, fruit fibre and peel from the syrup.

4   Let it cool for at least 10 minutes, then use in your gorgeous cocktails. This will last in the fridge for 2–3 weeks.

NOTE And save your peel! I have a great use for it on page 37.

ORANGE SYRUP

Makes about 450ml/15¾fl oz

Many gins have citrus notes, especially orange, in their flavour profiles, so the addition of orange syrup in a cocktail recipe feels like a natural match.

EQUIPMENT

chopping board
citrus juicer
hob
measuring jug
peeler
saucepan with lid
scales
sharp knife
storage container
strainer
wooden spoon

PROPORTIONS

2 parts sugar
1 part water

INGREDIENTS

2 oranges
300g/10oz caster (superfine) sugar
150ml/5fl oz water

1   Using a peeler, take the zest off the oranges, making sure that you don't take off the white pith underneath (doing so will make your syrup bitter). Put the zest in a saucepan with the sugar and water. Bring to the boil, then cover and simmer for 10 minutes, stirring occasionally to ensure the syrup doesn't burn. Remove from the heat.

2   Juice the oranges, then add the juice to the syrup and stir well.

3   Pour through a strainer into a sterilized airtight container so that you the separate pips, fruit, fibre and peel from the syrup.

4   Leave to cool for 10 minutes and use in your show-stopping cocktails. This will last in the fridge for 2–3 weeks.

NOTE And save your peel! I have a fantastic use for it on page 37. If you'd like to make this syrup with lemons, use three lemons with the same amount of sugar and water, but see Lemon and Thyme Syrup (below) for the best twist on lemon syrup.

LEMON & THYME SYRUP

Makes about 325ml/11fl oz

Never underestimate the power of herbs when making gin cocktails, they really can complement the botanicals in the gin beautifully. Lemon and thyme is a classic combination in cooking, so I decided to try it with my gin – and I was not disappointed.

EQUIPMENT

chopping board
citrus juicer
hob
peeler
saucepan with lid
scales
sharp knife
storage container
strainer
wooden spoon

PROPORTIONS

2 parts sugar
1 part water

INGREDIENTS

1 lemon
a handful of thyme (around 16 stalks of thyme about 10–12cm/4–4½in in length)
250g/9oz caster (superfine) sugar
180ml/6fl oz water

1. Using a peeler, take the zest off the lemon, making sure that you don't take off the white pith underneath (doing so will make your syrup bitter).

2. Put the thyme, lemon zest, sugar and water into a pan. Put the lid on the pan and bring to the boil, then simmer for 15 minutes, stirring occasionally to ensure the syrup doesn't burn. Remove from the heat. Put the lid back on and leave to stand for at least 2 hours, or longer for a more pronounced thyme flavour.

3. Juice the lemon and add the juice to the pan. Bring the syrup to the boil, then immediately take it off the heat.

4. Stir and pour through a strainer into a sterilized airtight container so that you separate pips, fruit fibre, peel and thyme from the syrup.

5. Let it cool, remove the peel and thyme stalks and use in your stunning cocktails. This will last in the fridge for 2–3 weeks.

LIME & BLACK PEPPER SYRUP
Makes about 400ml/14fl oz

Sometimes a grind of pepper can elevate a flavour to the next level, not just in cooking, but in drinks too. The vibrancy of lime complements gin beautifully and is delicious when made into a syrup. Add black pepper to the mix and you have an extra layer of brightness.

EQUIPMENT
chopping board
citrus juicer
hob
measuring jug
peeler
saucepan with lid
scales
sharp knife
storage container
wooden spoon

PROPORTIONS
2 parts sugar
1 part water

INGREDIENTS
4 limes
1 heaped teaspoon freshly
  milled black pepper
300g (10½oz) caster (superfine) sugar
150ml/5fl oz water

1. Using a peeler, take the zest off the limes, making sure that you don't take off the white pith underneath (doing so will make your syrup bitter).

2. Grind a heaped teaspoon of black pepper. Freshly milled black pepper has a lot more vibrancy and heat than pre-milled.

3. Put the zest and the pepper in a pan with the sugar and water. Bring to the boil, then cover and simmer for 10 minutes, stirring occasionally to ensure the syrup doesn't burn. Remove from the heat.

4. Juice the limes and add the juice to the syrup. Stir and pour through a strainer into a sterilized airtight container so that you separate pips, fruit fibre and peel from the syrup. (But don't worry if some pepper gets through – it looks really pretty, like flecks of vanilla in custard!)

5. Let the syrup cool for 10 minutes, then use in your show-stopping cocktails. Shake before serving. This will last in the fridge for 2–3 weeks.

ROSEMARY & BAY SYRUP

Makes about 250ml/8½fl oz

Rosemary is one of my favourite herbs to use in cooking, so I decided to introduce it to my cocktail making. Bay leaves add a certain charm to food and drink; they round out other flavours and act like a bridge, bringing them all together. The combination of the two works beautifully with cocktails, especially martinis. Don't be surprised by the deep pink colour. It was a shock to me. I noticed it forming when the rosemary was being infused towards the end of the process. However it happens, it's really pretty. So, enjoy the herbaceous flavour and gentle pink colour.

EQUIPMENT

hob
measuring jug
saucepan with lid
scales
storage container
strainer
wooden spoon

PROPORTIONS

1 part sugar
almost 1 part water

INGREDIENTS

5 dried bay leaves
5 black peppercorns
180ml/6fl oz water
200g/7oz caster (superfine) sugar
2 stalks of rosemary,
    about 12–14cm 4½–5½in in length

1 Break the bay leaves in half and put them into a saucepan along with the peppercorns, water and sugar. Put the lid on the pan and bring to the boil, then simmer for 15 minutes, stirring occasionally to ensure the syrup doesn't burn.

2 Remove from the heat. Leave to stand with the lid on for at least 2 hours (or longer for a more pronounced herbaceous flavour).

3 Add the rosemary, bring to the boil, then immediately take it off the heat. Stir and leave for 10 minutes.

4 Pour through a strainer into a sterilized airtight container so that you separate the bay leaves and rosemary from the syrup.

5 Let it cool, then use in your stunning cocktails. This will last in the fridge for 2–3 weeks.

RASPBERRY SYRUP

Makes about 350ml/12¼fl oz

If you like the fragrant vibrancy of raspberries as much as I do, you'll love this syrup. The natural intensity of flavour in a raspberry, coupled with its vibrant acidity, makes it perfect to turn into a syrup. As well as being great in cocktails, it's also wonderful over ice cream or sorbet!

EQUIPMENT

hob
masher, spatula, large spoon or large fork
measuring jug
saucepan
scales
storage container
strainer
wooden spoon

PROPORTIONS

3 parts raspberries
2 parts caster (superfine) sugar
2 parts water

INGREDIENTS

300g/10½oz raspberries
200g/7oz caster (superfine) sugar
200ml/7fl oz water

1   Bring a pan containing the raspberries, sugar and water to the boil. Once the mixture has come to the boil, turn it down and let it simmer for 25 minutes.

2   As it simmers, mash the raspberries with either a masher, a spatula, a large spoon or a large fork. Be sure to stir the mixture every few minutes or so to make sure it is not sticking. Also, make sure you don't allow the mixture to boil over. The raspberries have a tendency to froth up in the pan!

3   Take the syrup off the heat, and leave to cool for 10 minutes, then drain the mixture through a strainer into a sterilized airtight container, being sure to press the fruit pulp with a large spoon or spatula so you can extract as much liquid as you can. Note that the syrup will have a frothier texture than the other syrups due to the pulp being pushed through the strainer.

4   Once it has cooled, use in your delicious cocktails. This will last in the fridge for 2–3 weeks.

NOTE You can use frozen raspberries for this recipe. Just defrost them before making the syrup.

SHRUB IT UP!

A shrub is a syrup made with fruit, sugar and vinegar, the best vinegar being apple cider vinegar. A dash of shrub can be a lovely addition to your gin and tonic by adding a different flavour.

Rather than giving you a host of shrub recipes (which would be made using vinegar instead of water), feel free to adapt any of the flavoured fruit syrup recipes in this room by simply swapping out water for vinegar.

But if you'd like a cheat's shrub, take a measure of fruit-flavoured syrup, add an equal amount of vinegar and add it to your drink for a vibrant extra layer of fruit flavour.

When you use a shrub, the result is supposed to be bright and fruity. So, use the same amount of shrub as you'd use syrup. If you want more fruit in the finished cocktail, simply add a teaspoon of the neat syrup.

GARNISHES

Garnishes are fabulous. Even if a cocktail is sublime, the liquid itself might not always look as beautiful as it tastes, and that's where glassware and accessories can give your cocktails the wow factor.

I'll be honest, if I'm at home behind closed doors and it's just me and my hubby having a cocktail, I don't always bother with garnishes. (I'd rather spend the time fixing another round!) But they can bring a smile to your drinking partners' faces, so I'd like to share some ideas that will take your cocktails to the next level.

NOTE Oh, and just a little bit of housekeeping before we go on: please wash all fruit before use!

FRESH FRUIT

Fresh fruit can be a lovely addition to any cocktail and there are many ways that you can deploy it. Beyond, the humble fruit slice, wheel or wedge there are many fun ways to use fresh fruit as a garnish. From peeling to twisting to scorching, there's plenty you can do to mix up your accompaniments as you're mixing up your drink.

THE RINGLET

Probably the most universally smile-inducing cocktail garnish there is! This playful curl of citrus peel is such a lovely visual addition to any cocktail. It can also act as a flavour enhancer, as you can rub the oils round the rim of the glass.

EQUIPMENT

chopstick (optional)
peeler

INGREDIENTS

your choice of citrus fruit

1   Using a hand peeler, peel a ribbon of peel from the citrus fruit around 5cm/2in in length. From this, cut a full 5cm/2in length of peel which is around 2mm thick.

2   Using your fingers, twist the peel to make a ringlet shape. The peel is quite robust and can take the twist! If you are unsure of how to do this, twist the peel around a chopstick to form a ringlet and hold for 5 seconds. Slide off the chopstick and set aside.

3   Your ringlets can be made ahead of time and stored in the fridge to help them retain their shape. They may need a little reshaping when serving but this should be relatively easy, as long as you're not a few drinks down the line…

THE ROSE & THE RIBBON

Making citrus peel into a rose is an elegant way to add a bit of theatre to your cocktails. It is the work of moments and is easier than you think.

EQUIPMENT

cocktail stick
peeler

INGREDIENTS

your choice of citrus fruit

1   To make a citrus peel rose, use a peeler to peel a long ribbon of peel from the top to the bottom of the lemon. (To get good length, go around the lemon like a helter skelter.)

2   To create a rose, twist the lemon tightly so that the peel pulls into a rose shape and then pierce the end of the cocktail stick through the centre of the sides of the rose to hold in shape.

NOTE If you stop at the helter skelter, this can be used as a ribbon garnish, circling ice in a glass.

DRIED FRUIT

Drying fruit is a great way to make interesting garnishes. It is also a fantastic way to prepare your garnishes in advance. As well as this, drying fruit intensifies flavour and because it is dehydrated, the fruit isn't as heavy as when fresh so it will often float on top of a drink. And remember, dried fruit is your best friend if you're going somewhere without a fridge – like a picnic or a festival – and you want to garnish your drinks.

OVEN-DRIED FRUIT WHEELS

Using fruit wheels that have been oven dried is a great way to make your cocktails look sophisticated. As well as looking great garnishing your cocktails, they're also great to nibble on while you sip.

EQUIPMENT
chopping board
oven
oven tray
sharp knife

INGREDIENTS
your choice of citrus fruit or berry

1   Preheat the oven to 120°C/250°F (gas ½).

2   If using citrus fruit, cut your chosen citrus fruit in 2mm slices from one end to the other through the middle, revealing the wheel of segments. Lay your wheels on an oven tray and put into the oven, turning the fruit halfway through drying.

3   Approximate total timings are:
    limes – 50 minutes
    lemons – 12 hours
    clementines or similar – 2 hours
    oranges – 2 hours
    raspberries – 2 hours 10 minutes
    blackberries – 2 hours 10 minutes
    grapefruit – 2 hours 20 minutes.

NOTE All ovens are different and they can be temperamental, so check the fruit regularly to make sure that the peel is not burning. The peel will be ready when it is hard when tapped with a knife. The colour will darken – just don't let it turn black!

4   Loosen, if needs be, then leave to cool on the tray The fruit will go crisper as it cools. Put in an airtight container or zip-lock bag and keep in a cool dry place for up to 3 weeks.

5   You can float a wheel of dried citrus fruit on top of a cocktail just before serving or cut a slit from the middle to one end and slot on to the side of the glass. If drying berries, use a trio of them in the middle of the glass to make an elegant garnish.

OVEN-DRIED CITRUS PEEL CRISPS

Making these crisps is an interesting thing to do with citrus peel after you've made a sugar syrup (page 28). The sugar-coated pieces of peel are delicious with their huge intensity of flavour. They are great floated on top of a drink or ground into powder and put on the rim of your cocktail glass.

EQUIPMENT

oven
oven tray
spice grinder, pestle and mortar
  or rolling pin and food bag

INGREDIENTS

orange syrup (page 30)
your choice of citrus fruit

1   Preheat the oven to 110°C/225°F (gas ¼).

2   Follow step one of orange syrup (page 30) using your fruit of choice, then remove the syrup from the heat.

3   Drain the sugar syrup from the peel, separate the peel and lay it on an oven tray. Put in the oven for approximately 2 hours. Check the peel regularly to make sure that it is not burning, and turn halfway through. The peel will be ready when it is hard when tapped with a knife and will go crisper as it cools.

4   Leave to cool, then put in an airtight container or zip-lock bag and keep in a cool, dry place for up to 2 weeks.

5   Simply float a few crisps (depending on size) on top of your drinks and serve. Alternatively, crush in a pestle and mortar or blitz in a spice grinder to create a dust to sprinkle on top of your cocktails or to coat the rim of the glass (see below).

DUST OR CRUMB

I love serving a drink with a glass that has been treated to a decorative dust or crumb either in the centre of the surface of the drink or around the rim of a glass. It looks great and adds an extra layer of taste to the sensation of sipping the drink. You can crush hard-boiled sweets, dried fruit peel, dried banana or even biscuits or honeycomb to add a tasty treat to your cocktail. Here's how!

EQUIPMENT

2 small plates
pestle and mortar, spice grinder
  or a rolling pin and a food bag

INGREDIENTS

your choice of oven-dried citrus peel crisp,
  biscuit, honeycomb or boiled sweet
  (sherbet lemons are great!)

1   Using a pestle and mortar, spice grinder or a rolling pin and a food bag, grind or crush a handful of your chosen ingredient until it resembles breadcrumbs (for a crumb) or a powder (for dust).

2   A small pinch of this dust or crumb can be used as a garnish in the middle of the surface of a drink.

3   To decorate the rim of a glass, pour the powder onto a small plate. Put a splash of gin on another small plate and upturn your glasses onto the plate, ensuring that the circumference of each glass has been moistened with gin. (Do this quickly to avoid putting too much gin on the glass as this can result in dribbling.)

4   Immediately upturn the glass in the powder, ensuring the entire rim is covered (or you may prefer a half rim, it's up to you).

NOTE Make sure your plate is slightly wider than the circumference of your glass.

ICE CUBES

Frozen water is the simplest of ingredients and it is essential when stirring, shaking and serving many cocktails. But although an integral part of cocktail making, they tend to be functional rather than theatrical so why not help them move a little more centre stage? If you fancy getting adventurous, I've got some easy ways to make ice cubes look as stunning as the gin cocktails are to taste.

NOTE Ice cube trays come in all shapes and sizes, so use your own judgement in the amount of water and other ingredients that you use in these recipes.

RASPBERRY & MINT ICE CUBES

These ice cubes are so pretty. The red and green colours look great in cocktails all year round. The composition of fruit and leaf may look intricate, but they are so easy to make.

EQUIPMENT
chopping board
ice cube tray (with chambers
   around 2–3cm/¾–1¼in cubed)
kettle or saucepan
sharp knife

INGREDIENTS
water
raspberries
mint sprigs

1 Fill a kettle with water, boil the water, then leave to cool to room temperature. This will ensure that the water is less cloudy and clearer when frozen.

2 Place a raspberry upright in the middle of each ice cube chamber with the hull hole at the top.

3 Using the tops of the mint springs only (as they have a delicate collection of tiny leaves), pick the mint ends with your fingers and place your mint in the hull hole of the raspberry.

4 Carefully pour in the water, making sure that you don't displace the raspberry or mint (it's ok if the mint leaves are slightly sticking out of the water).

5 Place in a freezer and leave for at least 4 hours or until fully frozen (you should be familiar with the freezing times of your own freezer).

6 Serve only once fully frozen.

LEMON & THYME ICE CUBES

There's something so refreshing about the look of these ice cubes. The combination of lemon yellow and deep green looks like a lemon grove within the ice cube.

EQUIPMENT

chopping board
ice cube tray (with chambers
    around 4–5cm/1½–2in cubed)
kettle or saucepan
sharp knife

INGREDIENTS

water
lemon
thyme sprigs

1   Fill a kettle with water, boil the water, then leave to cool to room temperature. This will allow the water to be less cloudy and clearer when frozen.

2   Cut your lemon into 2mm thick half-moon wedges and place one diagonally in each ice cube chamber. (If it is tight, you can curl the lemon.)

3   Cut the thyme sprigs to the diagonal corner-to-corner length of your ice cube chambers. Place one sprig either side of your lemon slice.

4   Carefully pour in the water, making sure that you don't displace the lemon or thyme.

5   Place in a freezer and leave for at least 4 hours, or until fully frozen (you should be familiar with the freezing times of your own freezer).

6   Serve only once fully frozen.

CLEMENTINE ICE CUBES

Serving an ice cube with a perfectly sliced wheel of clementine in the middle is magical. I will certainly raise a smile from the person with the cocktail in hand. It is a two-stage process but it's worth it – after all, most of the work is being done once the ice cube is in the freezer!

Please note that this recipe will only be possible with an ice cube tray that makes large ice – the kind that you only need one piece of in your lowball glass. They will not fit in a collins or highball glass.

EQUIPMENT

chopping board
sharp knife
ice cube tray (with chambers
    around 5–6cm/2–2½in cubed)
kettle or saucepan

INGREDIENTS

water
clementine (or other small orange citrus fruit)

1   Make sure that you have the clementine the correct way around to display the full wheel of segments once cut. This means that the points of the fruit at either end should be facing out, not up or down. From one end of the fruit to the other, cut 2mm thick slices vertically.

The first and last few slices won't look great, but the others should look lovely in your ice cubes. Set aside.

2   Boil some water in a kettle or saucepan, then leave it to cool.

3   Half-fill your ice cube chambers with water and place a slice of clementine flat on top. (The clementine will float.) Freeze for at least 2 hours or until the half-completed ice cube has frozen. Take out of the freezer and fill up each chamber with the water.

4   Place back in the freezer and leave for at least 4 hours, or until fully frozen (you should be familiar with the freezing times of your own freezer).

5   Serve only once fully frozen.

CRANBERRY & ROSEMARY ICE CUBES

Cranberries are a wonderful fruit! They provide such flavour as an ingredient and make a superb juice drink. If you can't get fresh cranberries, use frozen, as they will be frozen in the ice cubes anyway! If you can't find frozen, dried will work just as well. The cranberry-red hue along with the dark green of the rosemary look great in cocktails all year round but are particularly special in winter because they look like baubles on a pine tree – fabulous in a G&T at Christmas.

EQUIPMENT

kettle or saucepan
ice cube tray (ideally with chambers around
2–3cm/¾–1¼in cubed if using one cranberry
per cube, or they can be bigger if using
several cranberries in one cube)

INGREDIENTS

cranberries
rosemary sprigs
water

1   Fill a kettle with water, boil the water, then leave it to cool to room temperature. This will allow the water to be less cloudy and clearer when frozen.

2   Half-fill your ice cube chambers with water and place a cranberry or cranberries on top. (The cranberries will float.) Pick sprigs containing 3 fronds of rosemary and place them around the cranberries. (Use your own judgement here – around 1–2 sprigs in small ice cubes or 3–4 in bigger ones.) Freeze for at least 2 hours or until the half-completed ice cube has frozen. Take out of the freezer and fill up each chamber with boiled water.

3   Place in the freezer and leave for at least 4 hours, or until fully frozen (you should be familiar with the freezing times of your own freezer).

4   Serve only once fully frozen.

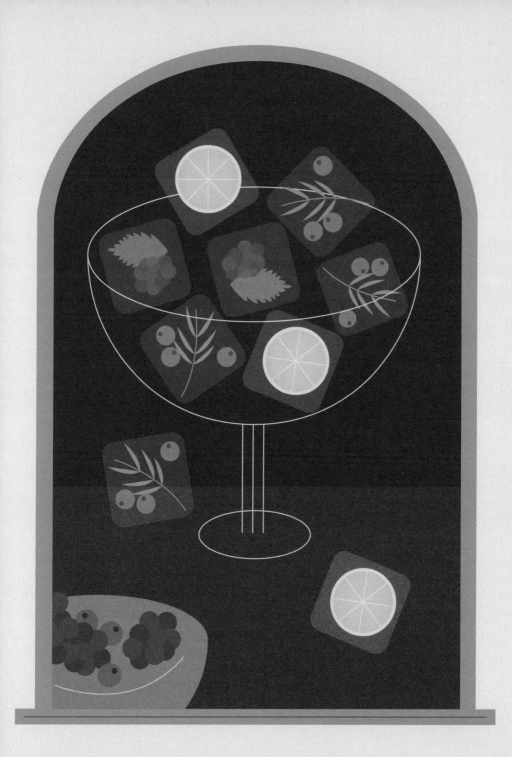

HOUSE CLASSICS

Classics are classics for a reason – there's something about these beauties that has allowed them to stand the test of time and remain resilient alongside changing tastes. I've recently reignited my love for the true gin classics and I've come to realize that you don't need to reinvent the wheel with every drink. I'm always eager to try new things and experiment, but sometimes it's great to take a breath and put your faith and your palate in the hands of those who have created some true gin-based gems.

These cocktails are from all over the world and have history in every sip, but they remain as bright and exciting today as they were the day they were conceived. Some are quite similar, as vibrant citrus in all its guises goes beautifully with the juniper-driven nature of gin. Find your favourites, enjoy them and by all means play with them (I have added a few of my own flourishes that aren't traditional when it comes to garnishes). After all, I am a firm believer that classic cocktails are there to be enjoyed in their purest form or with your own little twist!

You'll notice that a couple of gin classics – the gin ricky (page 114) and the French 75 (page 119) – are in the batch section of the book. This is because I want to show you that you can batch up a classic and share the love with many!

CLASSIC DRY GIN MARTINI

A gin martini is a time-honoured cocktail, essentially gin and dry white vermouth (which is a fortified aromatized wine – a great workhorse cocktail ingredient). It's not for everybody as, in its purest form, it contains no non-alcoholic mixer, therefore some find it too strong.

The most classic of the many variants and twists is the dry gin martini, 'dry' because most of it is dry gin. The ratio of gin to vermouth depends on the brands of liquor that you are using and individual taste, but here is my favourite option.

Some martini fans may want to chill the glasses in a freezer, and by all means do, but most of us don't have room. You can always rest some crushed ice in the glasses while preparing the cocktails, then empty the glasses before pouring, or store the liquids in the freezer.

PROPORTIONS

4 parts gin
1 part dry white vermouth

INGREDIENTS

a handful of ice
200ml/7fl oz gin
50ml/1¾ fl oz dry white vermouth
1 lemon

TO GARNISH

lemon peel ringlets (page 35)
  from the lemon in the ingredients

1   Make the lemon peel ringlets.

2   Put the ice and all liquid ingredients into a shaker. Shake for 20 seconds, or until the shaker is cold to the touch.

3   Strain into the glasses.

4   Take a small piece of lemon peel, twist it over the drink to release the oils and rub around the rim of the glass. Repeat with a fresh piece for the second glass.

5   Decorate each glass with a lemon peel ringlet.

NOTE   If you fancy a little twist, add a squeeze of lemon juice or why not put a couple of teaspoons of your favourite syrup into the cocktail?

EQUIPMENT

cocktail shaker	strainer
measuring jug	2 martini glasses

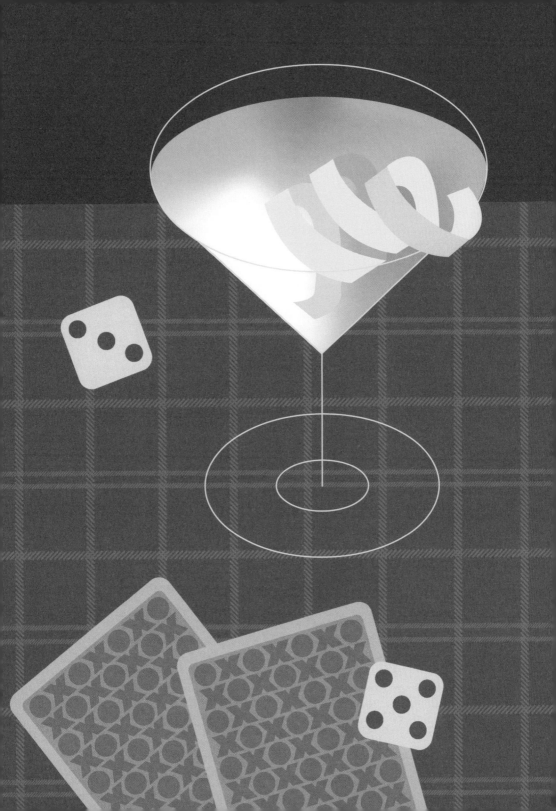

NEGRONI

The Negroni is a hugely popular Italian aperitif made from gin, vermouth rosso (red, semi-sweet or sweet vermouth), and Campari (or similar bitter liqueur). Traditionally it is stirred not shaken, to give a glassy, pure appearance and to avoid froth. Believed to have been created in Florence in the early 20th century, the Negroni has always had a presence on the cocktail lists at bars across the world, and I noticed it grew even more popular during the 2020 lockdown as people attempted easy-to-fix cocktails at home.

Like the dry martini, it is strong as there is no mixer, so you could add a dash of still water, tonic or soda to make a longer version if you find the cocktail too strong.

PROPORTIONS

1 part gin
1 part sweet red vermouth
1 part Campari

INGREDIENTS

75ml/2½fl oz gin
75ml/2½fl oz sweet red vermouth
75ml/2½fl oz Campari
  (or similar Italian style bitter)
a handful of ice
a strip of orange peel

TO GARNISH

2 clementine ice cubes (page 39)

1   Put the gin, vermouth and Campari into a jug along with a handful of ice. Stir gently.

2   Put the clementine ice cubes in the glasses and then pour the cocktail into the glasses.

3   Take a small piece of orange peel, twist it over the drink to release the oils and rub around the rim of the glass. Repeat with a fresh piece for the second glass.

4   Decorate each drink with an orange peel ringlet.

EQUIPMENT

jug
peeler

stirrer
2 lowball glasses

GIN FIZZ

Of an evening, I can easily sip a couple of G&Ts one after the other, but then I want to change it up a bit and the gin fizz is a great cocktail when you decide you want to move on. The brightness of the lemon juice and the dash of sweetness from the simple sugar syrup makes me smile.

It is thought that cocktails involving gin and fizz date back to the mid 18th century but it's the version created by Henry Charles Ramos (also known as Carl) at the Imperial Cabinet Saloon in New Orleans, Louisiana in 1888 that got people talking. It is believed that double (heavy) cream was used for texture.

Since then, tastes have changed so I'm sharing with you a version that uses an egg white for texture.

PROPORTIONS

4 parts gin
2 parts lemon juice
1 part simple sugar syrup
12 parts sparkling water

INGREDIENTS

100ml/3½fl oz gin
50ml/1¾fl oz lemon juice
25ml/1½ tbsp simple sugar syrup (page 28)
1 egg white
a handful of ice
300ml/10fl oz sparkling water

TO GARNISH

2 handfuls of ice
2 half-moon lemon slices

1   Put the gin, lemon juice, syrup and egg white into the shaker. Shake for 10 seconds. The drink should now appear frothy.

2   Release the lid and add a handful of ice, then shake for 20 seconds more, or until the shaker is cold to the touch.

3   Fill the glasses with ice, place the half-moon slices of lemon amongst the ice and strain the contents of the shaker into the glasses. Top up with sparkling water to taste.

NOTE   If you want to change it up, why not try a citrus syrup (pages 29–30) or a citrus gin. Orange gin can work a treat.
If you like, you can add a few drops of orange blossom water for extra fragrance, but I don't feel that the recipe needs it.

EQUIPMENT

cocktail shaker   strainer
measuring jug   2 highball glasses

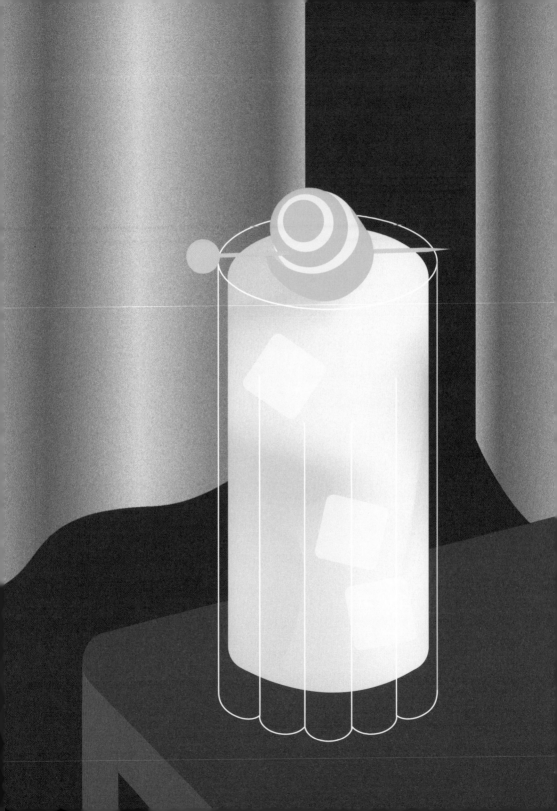

TOM COLLINS

Tom Collins is a name that is synonymous with gin. There is enough history surrounding the drink and its name to write an essay, but essentially there are differing origins for this drink. One is that the Tom Collins originated as the John Collins in London in the 1860s. Another suggests that it was created by a different Mr Collins in a New York tavern in the 1870s. The third revolves around the 'Great Tom Collins Hoax of 1874' where people in the cities of New York and Philadelphia were tricked into thinking that Tom Collins was a bar-dwelling man with a bit of an attitude towards others, only to find out that he didn't actually exist but a cocktail bearing his name did. (I know, it's all a bit complicated!)

Anyhow, you're not going mad if you look at this recipe and you see that it's pretty much the same as the Gin Fizz because it's basically the same thing in a different glass! I don't believe Tom Collins recipes use egg like many gin fizz recipes, so I've omitted the egg white that I used in the previous recipe so that you can see and taste the subtle difference for yourself.

PROPORTIONS

4 parts gin
12 parts sparkling water
2 parts lemon juice
1 part simple sugar syrup

INGREDIENTS

a handful of ice
100ml/3½fl oz gin
300ml/10fl oz sparkling water
50ml/¾fl oz lemon juice
25ml/1½ tbsp simple sugar syrup (page 28)

TO GARNISH

2 handfuls of ice
2 lemon peel roses (page 35)

1   Make the lemon peel rose.

2   Put all liquid ingredients into a jug along with a handful of ice. Stir gently.

3   Add some ice cubes to the glasses, then pour in the cocktail.

4   Decorate each glass with a lemon peel rose.

NOTE   If you fancy a little twist, add a squeeze of lemon juice or why not put a couple of teaspoons of your favourite syrup into the cocktail.

EQUIPMENT

jug
measuring jug

stirrer
2 Collins glasses

SINGAPORE SLING

I first fell in love with this world-famous cocktail after a conversation with the hugely successful British businessperson, Deborah Meaden, when we appeared on ITV's lifestyle show *Love your Weekend with Alan Titchmarsh* where I was preparing Easter cocktails. She told me it was her all-time favourite cocktail.

The Singapore Sling was first created in 1915 at The Long Bar in the famous Raffles Hotel by Ngiam Tong Boon. Upon researching more about the recipe I discovered many variants! Gin and Benedictine (a French herbal liqueur) seem to be the ingredients that are a constant, but some of the others come and go depending on which recipe you're looking at. Some use pineapple juice, some use grenadine (berry-based syrup), some use sparkling water and some recipes don't use any of these ingredients! In the face of confusion, I scribbled down my own ideas on how I thought it should taste – and it worked first time! It tastes tropical and fun – just like you're on holiday at an exclusive hotel.

PROPORTIONS

1 part gin
1 part Benedictine
1 part cherry brandy
1 part lime juice
1 part pineapple juice

INGREDIENTS

a handful of ice
100ml/3½fl oz gin
100ml/3½fl oz Benedictine
100ml/3½fl oz cherry brandy
100ml/3½fl oz lime juice
100ml/3½fl oz pineapple juice

GARNISH

2 handfuls of ice
2 dashes of bitters
2 edible flowers (preferably a nasturtium or a small edible pansy)

1   Put the ice and all the liquid ingredients into a shaker. Shake for 20 seconds, or until the shaker is cold to the touch.

2   Fill the glasses with ice, strain the cocktail into the glasses and decorate with the bitters and edible flowers.

EQUIPMENT

cocktail shaker
strainer
2 hurricane glasses

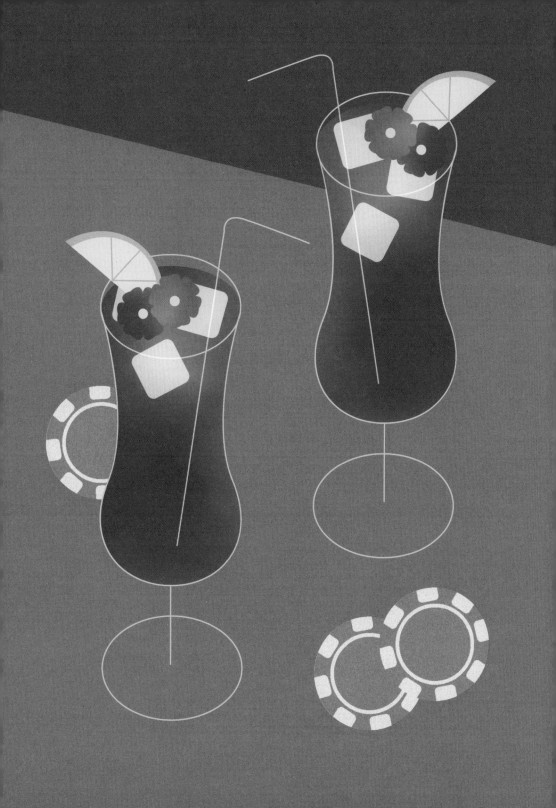

CLOVER CLUB

It's easy to forget the classics. I can't tell you the number of times I've overlooked the Clover Club on a cocktail list in favour of something new. If you have done the same, I urge you not to do it on this occasion.

This delicious pre-Prohibition cocktail first came to prominence in Philadelphia in the 1880s at the Bellevue-Stratford Hotel and was named after a men's club of the same name who regularly met at the hotel.

The clover club is an exciting and fruity cocktail that shows the beauty of gin in the best way. Citrus and berry sweetness elevate the vibrancy and charisma of gin.

PROPORTIONS

3 parts gin
2 parts lemon juice
1 part raspberry syrup

INGREDIENTS

a handful of ice
150ml/5fl oz gin
100ml/3½fl oz lemon juice
50ml/1½fl oz raspberry syrup (page 33)
1 egg white

GARNISH

6 dried raspberries (page 36)

1   Put the ice and all the liquid ingredients into a shaker. Shake for 20 seconds, or until the shaker is cold to the touch, then strain into the glasses.

2   Place three dried raspberries on top of the drink in a triangle formation in the middle and serve.

EQUIPMENT

cocktail shaker
strainer
2 coupe glasses

BRAMBLE

Following the tradition of citrus and berries complementing gin, the bramble was created in 1984, making it more of a modern classic. (Well, I think of anything within my lifetime as being relatively modern!) It was created by bartender Dick Bradsell who was working at a bar in London's Soho called Fred's Club. His genius marriage of lemon and blackberry is delightful, especially when paired with a beautiful citrus and juniper-led gin and the theatricality of the crème de mûre top is a smile inducer!

PROPORTIONS

4 parts gin
2 parts lemon juice
1 part simple sugar syrup
1 part crème de mûre

INGREDIENTS

a handful of ice
100ml/3½fl oz gin
50ml/¾fl oz lemon juice
25ml/1½ tbsp simple sugar syrup (page 28) or raspberry syrup (page 33)
25ml/1½ tbsp crème de mûre

GARNISH

6 blackberries
2 handfuls of crushed ice

1   To make your garnish, thread 3 blackberries on each cocktail stick and set aside.

2   Put the handful of ice, the gin, lemon juice and syrup into a shaker. Shake for 20 seconds, or until the shaker is cold to the touch.

3   Add the crushed ice to the glasses and strain the contents of the shaker into the glasses. Evenly distribute the crème de mûre on top and let it dissipate down through the drinks, creating a beautiful two-toned effect.

4   Place the blackberries on the cocktail stick across the rim of the glasses and serve.

NOTE   If you can't find crème de mûre, any other blackberry liqueur will work. And if you want more berry flavour, you could use sloe gin, just balance out with a dash more lemon juice to make sure it's not too sweet. Also, if you are feeling adventurous, you could swap out the fresh blackberries for dried ones. And if you fancy turning your cocktail into a 'Bramble Royale', simply add a generous splash of dry sparkling wine before you add the crème de mûre.

EQUIPMENT

cocktail shaker
strainer

2 cocktail sticks
2 lowball glasses

CORPSE REVIVER NO. 2

I know what your first question is: Where's No. 1?!

Well, I can answer that pretty swiftly: No. 1 is not a gin-based cocktail. No. 2 is a gin-based cocktail (obviously, otherwise it wouldn't be in this book)!

But why is it called a corpse reviver? There are references going back to the 1860s to 'corpse reviver' cocktails, which were always pretty potent and punchy drinks that could metaphorically revive a corpse! But a corpse reviver inclusion in one of my favourite cocktail books – Harry Craddock's *The Savoy Cocktail Book* published in 1930 – brought attention to Corpse reviver no. 1 (consisting of cognac, calvados, sweet red vermouth and water) and No. 2, which you can see here. Happy reviving!

PROPORTIONS

2 parts gin
2 parts triple sec
2 parts lemon juice
2 parts dry white vermouth

INGREDIENTS

a handful of ice
75ml/2½fl oz gin
75ml/2½fl oz triple sec
75ml/2½fl oz lemon juice
75ml/2½fl oz dry white vermouth
(traditionally Lillet Blanc)
a swill or 1 tsp absinthe
2 strips of lemon peel

GARNISH

2 lemon peel ringlets (page 35)

1   Put the ice and all the liquid ingredients into a shaker. Shake for 20 seconds, or until the shaker is cold to the touch. Strain into the glasses.

2   Take a small piece of lemon peel, twist it over the drink to release the oils, then rub around the rim of the glass. Repeat with a fresh piece for the second glass, then discard the peel.

3   Decorate each glass with a lemon peel ringlet.

NOTE If you fancy a little twist, add a squeeze of lemon juice or why not add a couple of teaspoons of your favourite syrup to the cocktail.

EQUIPMENT

cocktail shaker
measuring jug
peeler

strainer
2 coupe glasses

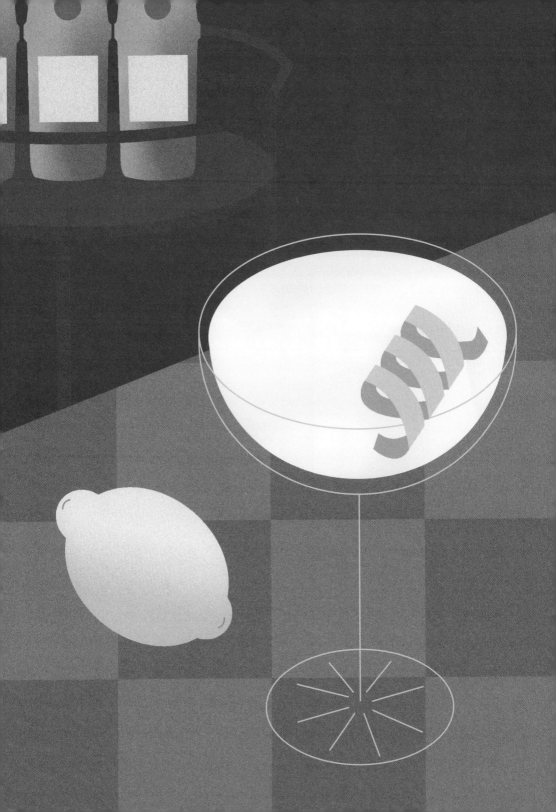

MAKES	GIN TYPES	FLAVOURS	SEASONS
2 servings	Sloe • berry • damson	rich • ripe berry • stone fruit	summer • winter

CHARLIE CHAPLIN

This classic gin cocktail is the perfect use for the vibrant berry notes of sloe gin. Created in the early 20th century at New York City's Waldorf Astoria hotel during the lifetime of silent film actor Charlie Chaplin, like the movies, it has not remained popular with the advent of more modern cocktails. However, in my opinion this cocktail is the perfect marriage of all these ingredients.

I love apricot brandy as an ingredient but ... stop press! There is a big difference between using an apricot brandy or an apricot liqueur. Apricot brandy has a lot more depth of flavour and richness. Apricot liqueur can be much sweeter.

Also, sloe gins can differ in fruit richness and sugar content so make sure you scribble the details of your favourite on this page and find your Charlie.

PROPORTIONS

3 parts sloe gin
3 parts apricot brandy (2 parts if using a non-brandy apricot liqueur)
2 parts lime juice

INGREDIENTS

a handful of ice
75ml/2½fl oz sloe gin
75ml/2½fl oz apricot brandy
  (or 50ml/1½fl oz if using a non-brandy apricot liqueur)
50ml/1½fl oz lime juice

GARNISH

2 orange peel ringlets (page 35)

1   Put the ice and all the liquid ingredients into a shaker. Shake for 20 seconds, or until the shaker is cold to the touch, and then strain into the glasses.

2   Decorate each glass with an orange peel ringlet.

NOTE   You could also use your favourite berry gin here, but make sure that the gin has a certain level of sweetness otherwise the cocktail will be too sharp.

EQUIPMENT

cocktail shaker
strainer
2 Nick & Nora glasses

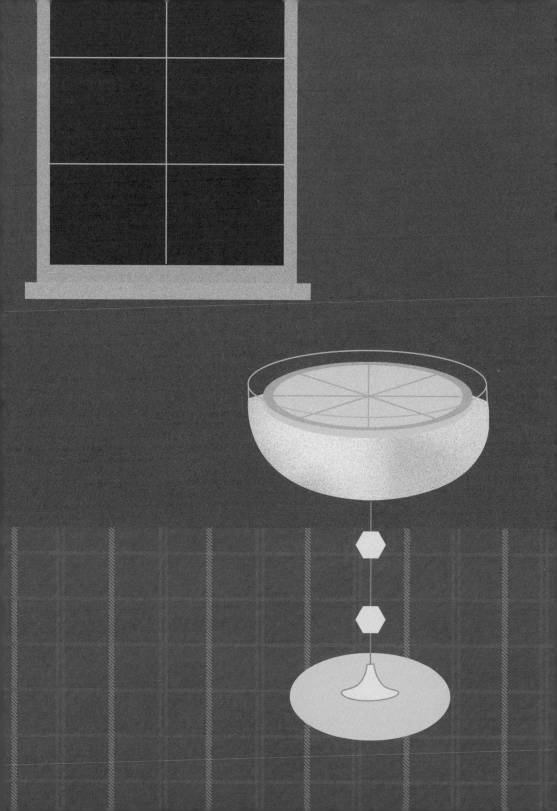

GIMLET

I love the simplicity of a gimlet. It displays elegance and allows good gin to shine. Created by a surgeon, not a bartender, it is said that surgeon Rear-Admiral Sir Thomas Gimlette added lime to gin to help combat scurvy during lengthy sea voyages in the 19th century. British sailors were provided with lime rations in an effort to combat scurvy, the juice of which was often turned into drinks, so it seems fitting that the gimlet was created in this way.

Traditionally, the drink is made using lime cordial, but I am much more a fan of a fresher, zingier taste using fresh lime juice.

I know the cocktail may have been created by Mr Gimlette, but I wonder if the cocktail is named after the 'gimlet' tool designed for drilling small holes into wood? (After all, the first sip provides more than a little poke!)

PROPORTIONS

4 parts gin
2 parts lime juice
1 part simple sugar syrup

INGREDIENTS

a handful of ice
200ml/7fl oz gin
100ml/3½fl oz lime juice
50ml/1½fl oz simple sugar syrup (page 28)

GARNISH

2 fresh lime wheels

1   Put the ice, gin, lime juice and syrup into a shaker. Shake for 20 seconds, or until the shaker is cold to the touch, and then strain into the glasses.

2   Decorate the glasses with the lime wheels.

NOTE   If you want a hint of Rose's lime cordial about the drink, use 3 parts gin rather than 4. And if you'd like to up the zingy lime charge, use lime & black pepper syrup (page 31). Or to add a herbaceous citrus layer, use the lemon & thyme syrup (page 30).

EQUIPMENT

cocktail shaker
measuring jug

strainer
2 coupe glasses

BEE'S KNEES

I love using sweeteners that add character to cocktails. There is a place for simple sugar syrup, especially in classic cocktail recipes, but any opportunity I get to use flavoured sweeteners, I will. So, the bee's knees is a delight! Honey syrup provides a rich and rounded sweetness that works beautifully with gin.

The 'bee's knees' is an expression that describes something of excellence, and as honey is made by bees, it seems only fitting that it has that name!

As often happens with classic cocktails, the origin of bee's knees is unclear. Some say the cocktail was invented by Frank Meier, head bartender at the Ritz in Paris in 1921. Others put it down to American Socialite Margaret Brown, known as 'The Unsinkable Molly Brown' as she was a *Titanic* survivor. There are also rumours of the cocktail having been developed in the USA during Prohibition. Whoever gave this a go first, I think you'll love the dreamy blend of gin, honey and lemon.

PROPORTIONS

2 parts gin
1 part lemon juice
1 part honey syrup

INGREDIENTS

a handful of ice
150ml/5fl oz gin
75ml/2½fl oz lemon juice
75ml/2½fl oz Honey Syrup (page 29)

GARNISH

1 sherbet lemon boiled sweet
  for the dusty rim (page 37)

1   Make your sherbet lemon dust and garnish the glasses.

2   Put the ice and all the liquid ingredients into a shaker. Shake for 20 seconds, or until the shaker is cold to the touch, and then strain into the glasses.

EQUIPMENT

cocktail shaker
measuring jug
strainer

spice grinder or
  pestle and mortar
2 Nick & Nora glasses

SOUTHSIDE

Known as a kind of gin mojito because of the influence of lime and mint, this cocktail is a refreshing but short cocktail. To make it even more mojito-like you could make a longer version with a dash of sparkling water over ice. But which southside is this cocktail named after? The cocktail has origins in the pre-Prohibition era. Was it invented at the Southside Sportsmen's Club on Long Island? Or is it linked to Chicago's Southside where Al Capone and his gang needed to temper the burn of harsh gin? Whether you're sipping your cocktail on the northside, the southside or anywhere in between, enjoy this unique and refreshing combination of lime, mint and (hopefully smooth) gin!

PROPORTIONS

2 parts gin
1 part lime juice
1 part simple sugar syrup

INGREDIENTS

a small handful of mint
150ml/5fl oz gin
a handful of ice
75ml/2½fl oz lime juice
75ml/2½fl oz simple sugar syrup (page 28)

GARNISH

2 sprigs of mint
2 dried lime wheels (page 36)

1   In the shaker, muddle the mint with the gin until the mint has broken up and you can smell mint when your face is close to the shaker.

2   Add the ice and all other liquid ingredients. Shake for 20 seconds, or until the shaker is cold to the touch, and then strain into the glasses. (If you are using a fine mesh strainer, allow some of the mint flecks to come out as they look really pretty in the glass.)

3   Decorate each drink with a sprig of mint and the lime discs lying flat on top of the drink.

NOTE   If you fancy a more fragrant version, try using honey syrup (page 29) instead of simple sugar syrup.

EQUIPMENT

cocktail shaker   strainer
measuring jug   2 coupe glasses
muddler

AVIATION

OK, the flavours of violet and cherry aren't for everybody, which is possibly why the aviation may have waned in popularity since it was first created in the pre-Prohibition world of the early 20th century. I rather like the salute to the flavours of childhood 'after-school' penny sweets that we'd buy from the corner shop on the way home. (Obvs without alcohol!)

It would seem that the name of this cocktail is a nod to the growing aeronautical industry of the time and possibly the pale sky-like colour of the drink. There are versions of this that don't contain crème de violette, most notably Harry Craddock's version in *The Savoy Cocktail Book*, but I feel that it's essential for the unique overall colour and flavour of the cocktail.

PROPORTIONS

4 parts gin
3 parts lemon juice
2 parts maraschino liqueur
1 part crème de violette

INGREDIENTS

a handful of ice
100ml/3½fl oz gin
75ml/2½fl oz lemon juice
50ml/1½fl oz maraschino liqueur
25ml/1½ tbsp crème de violette

GARNISH

2 edible flowers (preferably a small purple edible pansy) OR 2 maraschino cherries on cocktail sticks

1   Put the ice and all liquid ingredients in a cocktail shaker. Shake for 20 seconds, or until the shaker is cold to the touch, and then strain into the glasses.

2   Garnish with the edible flowers. (But if you want to go classic, thread two maraschino cherries on to cocktail sticks and dip in the drinks.)

EQUIPMENT

cocktail shaker
measuring jug
strainer

2 coupe glasses
2 cocktail sticks
   (optional)

LOUD SPEAKER

The title of this classic cocktail made me smile as it reminded me of the type of cocktail I might sip after coming off stage or finishing in the studio. It also contains some of my favourite ingredients. I discovered it in *The Savoy Cocktail Book*, and it had this description by author Harry Craddock:

'This it is that gives to radio announcers their peculiar enunciation. Three of them will produce oscillation, and after five it is possible to reach the osculation stage.'

I have to be honest, I had to look up what osculation means! And according to vocabulary. com, 'it's a fancy way of saying "kiss", and if you think it sounds vaguely mathematical, you're right. Osculation is also a term in geometry that describes the place where two curves or surfaces come into contact, or where their common tangent exists. It's almost as if the two curved lines are kissing.'

PROPORTIONS

2 parts gin
2 parts brandy
1 part triple sec
1 part lemon juice

INGREDIENTS

a handful of ice
100ml/3½fl oz gin
100ml/3½fl oz brandy (preferably Cognac)
50ml/1½fl oz triple sec (Cointreau)
50ml/1½fl oz lemon juice

GARNISH

2 orange peel ringlets (page 35)

1   Put the ice and all the liquid ingredients into a shaker. Shake for 20 seconds, or until the shaker is cold to the touch, and then strain into the glasses.

2   Decorate each glass with an orange peel ringlet.

EQUIPMENT

cocktail shaker
measuring jug

strainer
2 Nick & Nora glasses

LAST WORD

It seems fitting that the final cocktail in this classics section is the last word. It's one of my favourite gin classics. The cocktail was first served at the Detroit Athletic Club around the same time as Prohibition started in 1920 (some say just before, some say just after). It's not a cocktail that has been prominent or fashionable on cocktail lists in my adult life, but I think it's a bit of a forgotten classic that deserves to shine once more.

The unique blend of gin, the distinctively herbaceous French liqueur green chartreuse and the rich cherry charms of maraschino liqueur is a fabulous combination when introduced to lime juice. And the real test is that whilst chartreuse and strong cherry flavours would not be my husband's favourite flavours, he loves this cocktail, which is a very good test of this old school beauty (the cocktail, not him).

PROPORTIONS

1 part gin
1 part green chartreuse
1 part maraschino liqueur
1 part lime juice

INGREDIENTS

a handful of ice
50ml/1½fl oz gin
50ml/1½fl oz green chartreuse
50ml/1½fl oz maraschino liqueur
50ml/1½fl oz lime juice

GARNISH

2 sprigs of rosemary

1   Put the ice and all the liquid ingredients into a shaker. Shake for 20 seconds, or until the shaker is cold to the touch, and then strain into the glasses.

2   Decorate each glass with a sprig of rosemary.

EQUIPMENT
cocktail shaker
strainer
2 Nick & Nora glasses

HOUSE SPECIALS

I love getting creative with cocktails. I'm happiest when surrounded by bottles with very little plan – I just see where my mood and the ingredients take me. When it comes to gin cocktails, I have the most fun experimenting with flavour. It's important to respect the profile of gin with all the delicate and complex notes different gins give.

Part of the beauty of cocktail experimentation is that I don't always get it right – but when I do, I'm jumping up and down with joy and I can't wait to share my concoctions with others. So, here are a few house specials that provide a new take on gin.

In this house, there are no rules. Let's just push the boundaries and have fun!

ROOM 6
THE LOUNGE

G & TEA MARTINI

When not sipping gin, I can often be found sipping tea. I love putting the kettle on in the morning and having that first strong cup of black breakfast tea with a dash of milk. (I favour a wonderful Irish brand called Barry's Tea. My Irish husband introduced it to me when we first met and I can't get enough of it!) The many varieties of tea can also make a great cocktail ingredient; pick your favourite and you'll easily be able to work it into a cocktail.

Whilst filming a UK daytime television programme called *Love your Weekend with Alan Titchmarsh*, I met Katherine Jenkins, the internationally renowned operatic mezzo-soprano. As we are both huge gin fans, we decided to make some reels of us making cocktails for social media using her delicious Cygnet Gin from South Wales. As part of this, we knew we really wanted to show how to make a martini. I'm all for creating twists, but it was Katherine's idea to try adding the relaxing, floral flavours of chamomile tea to the cocktail, so I made a cup of chamomile tea and decided to experiment making the drink for the first time on camera. It worked first time and we loved it!

Here is my recipe for a G & Tea Martini, inspired by Katherine. *Lechyd da*!

PROPORTIONS

4 parts gin
2 parts chamomile tea
1 part dry white vermouth

INGREDIENTS

a handful of ice
200ml/7fl oz gin
100ml/3½fl oz chamomile tea
   made from 1 teabag
50ml/1½fl oz dry white vermouth
2 tsp honey syrup (page 29)

TO GARNISH

2 lemon peel roses (page 35)

1   Put the teabag in a mug. Using the kettle, heat the water to boiling. Pour the boiling water on the teabag, and give it a stir with the teaspoon. (A mug will hold around 275ml/9fl oz so use around that amount of water.) After 5 minutes, remove the teabag. Allow to cool to room temperature.

2   Once the tea has cooled, put the ice and all the liquid ingredients into a shaker. Shake for 20 seconds, or until the shaker is cold to touch, and then strain into the glasses.

3   Garnish each glass with a lemon peel rose balanced on the rim of the glass, crossing the glass in two places.

NOTE If you'd like more of a herbaceous note to complement the flavours of this cocktail, use rosemary & bay syrup (page 32) instead of honey syrup. Also, if chamomile is not your thing, use whatever tea you like to sip.

EQUIPMENT

cocktail shaker	strainer
dessert spoon	teaspoon
kettle	2 cocktail sticks
mug	2 martini glasses

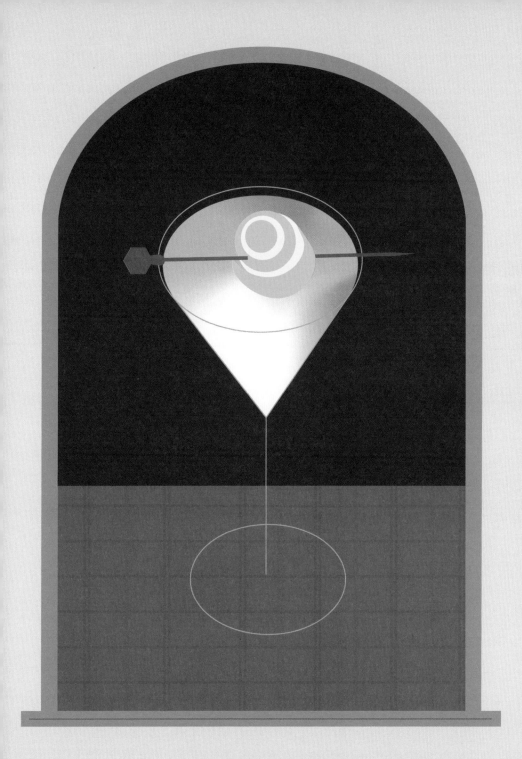

VICTORY SPRITZ

I created a version of this cocktail for Rugby Distillery based in the town where the sport was invented by William Webb Ellis whilst he was a student at Rugby School. The distillery created a gin using lemons from Menton, the French town on the Mediterranean coast where William passed away. If you have a lemon gin, feel free to use it here but as there is lemon juice in the cocktail, it's not essential. Just make sure you use a gin that exudes citrus, as the raspberry cordial and cucumber tonic water will work so well with this kind of gin.

I created the cocktail to celebrate the rugby world cup, but you don't have to be a rugby fan to like this cocktail. I encourage you to sip this as you cheer on your home team, whatever the sport!

PROPORTIONS

4 parts gin
8 parts cucumber tonic water
1 part raspberry syrup
2 parts lemon juice

INGREDIENTS

a handful of ice
2 handfuls of raspberry
  & mint ice cubes (page 38)
100ml/3½fl oz gin
200ml/7fl oz cucumber tonic water
25ml/1½ tbsp raspberry syrup (page 33)
50ml/1½fl oz lemon juice

GARNISH

1 sherbet lemon boiled sweet
  for the dusty rim (page 37)

a sprig of mint (optional)

1   Make your sherbet lemon dust and garnish the glasses.

2   Put a handful of ice into the jug and add all the liquid ingredients. Stir gently. Fill your glasses with the raspberry & mint ice cubes and pour in the cocktail. Serve immediately, garnish with mint if using, and support your team!

NOTE If you don't want to make the ice cubes, use normal ice and pop a few raspberries into the glasses when filling them with ice. Decorate with a sprig of mint.

EQUIPMENT

jug
measuring jug
stirrer

spice grinder or
  pestle and mortar
2 highball glasses

RASPBERRY GIN SOUR

I'm a big fan of a sour. The zing of citrus complements many spirits, but it is particularly great with gin. I love a short, strong drink with a citrus bite and I'm adding this to the list of my favourite short gin drinks. This is what I call a 3-2-1 recipe because of the proportions of the liquid ingredients. It's a good way to remember how to make it!

Based on the idea of a clover club, I've used lime juice instead of lemon for a vibrant green edge to complement the raspberry flavour and I've added bitters to give extra hints of clove and cinnamon.

PROPORTIONS

3 parts gin
2 parts lime juice
1 part raspberry syrup

INGREDIENTS

150ml/5fl oz gin
100ml/3½fl oz lime juice
50ml/1½fl oz raspberry syrup (page 33)
1 egg white
a handful of ice
a generous shake of bitters
(around 2 teaspoons)

GARNISH

6 dried raspberries (page 36)
2 sprigs of mint

1   Add the gin, lime juice, raspberry syrup and the egg white to the shaker. Shake for 10 seconds until the drink appears frothy. Release the lid and add a handful of ice, then shake for 20 seconds more, or until the shaker is cold to the touch.

2   Strain the cocktail into the glasses. Decorate each glass with 3 dried raspberries in the centre of the surface of each cocktail and put a sprig of mint in the centre.

EQUIPMENT

cocktail shaker
measuring jug

strainer
2 coupe glasses

THE GRAND LADY IN A SIDECAR

The white lady is an epically beautiful classic cocktail. The punchy combo of gin, bittersweet orange triple sec and zingy lemon juice is a real gem. I'm also a lover of a sidecar, the cocktail named after the motorcycle attachment, which was very commonly used back when the cocktail was invented in the early 20th century, consisting of Cognac, triple sec and lemon juice.

Orange brandy liqueur is a wonderful thing and Grand Marnier is one of my absolute favourites, so by substituting triple sec for orange brandy I've created something that is in between a white lady and a sidecar. This cheeky yet elegant cocktail will knock your socks off and give you kick at the same time. Just make sure you're given a lift home (preferably in a sidecar) after you've had a couple of these!

PROPORTIONS

2 parts gin
2 parts Grand Marnier
  (or other orange brandy)
1 part lemon juice

INGREDIENTS

100ml/3½fl oz gin
100ml/3½fl oz Grand Marnier
  (or other orange brandy)
50ml/1½fl oz lemon juice
1 egg white
a handful of ice

GARNISH

2 orange peel ringlets (page 35)

1   Put all the liquid ingredients into the shaker along with the egg white. Shake for 10 seconds. The drink should now have a slightly frothy texture.

2   Release the lid and add the handful of ice, then shake for 20 seconds more or until the shaker is cold to the touch.

3   Strain into the glasses. Garnish with the orange peel ringlets and serve.

NOTE If you'd like this cocktail slightly sweeter, after tasting, add a teaspoon of honey syrup (page 29) to each glass.

EQUIPMENT

cocktail shaker
measuring jug
strainer

2 dessert
  wine glasses

THE BEE'S MEAD

This cocktail is a celebration of bees! One of the world's greatest assets. A twist on the bee's knees cocktail (page 64), which uses honey syrup as a sweetener, this version uses mead, an ancient drink made by fermenting honey with water. It's an easy way to achieve the charm of a bee's knees without having to make the honey syrup. It's a three-ingredient beauty that will please your palate in the most delightful way. But if, like me, you're not keen on overly sweet cocktails, don't let the honey element put you off, the lemon juice is perfectly poised to balance out the honeyed notes and let the gin shine. Remember that different meads will have different sweetness and honey concentrations, so if you really like honey, after tasting, you may want to add a teaspoon of honey syrup (page 29) to each glass.

PROPORTIONS

2 parts gin
3 parts mead
1 part lemon juice

INGREDIENTS

a handful of ice
100ml/3½fl oz gin
150ml/5fl oz mead
50ml/1½fl oz lemon juice

GARNISH

1 piece of honeycomb,
about 2cm/¾in cubed

1   To crush the honeycomb, use a pestle and mortar or a rolling pin and a food bag until you have small shards that will float on top of the finished cocktail.

2   Put the ice and all the liquid ingredients into a shaker. Shake for 20 seconds, or until the shaker is cold to the touch, and then strain into the glasses. Garnish with a pinch of honeycomb over the surface of each cocktail.

NOTE   Make sure that you are using still mead and not a sparkling version, otherwise the contents of your shaker will explode.

EQUIPMENT

cocktail shaker
pestle and mortar

strainer
2 coupe glasses

GARDEN PARTY BUBBLY

Believe me, from experience, a cocktail comprising dry sparkling wine and lemon juice is going to go down really well when hosting an al fresco party.

This cocktail is based on the French 75, which traditionally consists of gin, Champagne, lemon juice and simple sugar syrup, but I'm changing things up a bit (to make the classic French 75, turn to page 119).

For a start, don't feel you have to use Champagne. I encourage you to find a local dry sparkling wine that you like and use it in the drink. I always think it's important to support local producers. Also, by adding lemon and thyme syrup, the cocktail gets an extra layer of lemon along with a rounded herbaceous note – perfect for an outdoor do!

PROPORTIONS

15 parts dry sparkling wine
6 parts gin
2 parts lemon juice
2 parts lemon & thyme syrup

INGREDIENTS

a large handful of ice
750ml bottle dry sparkling wine
200ml/7fl oz gin
100ml/3½fl oz lemon juice
100ml/3½fl oz lemon & thyme syrup
  (page 30)

GARNISH

10 sprigs of thyme
dashes of orange bitters

1   Put the ice into the jug. Add the gin, lemon juice and syrup.

2   Open the dry sparkling wine and gently add to the jug, slowly pouring with the jug on an angle so it doesn't froth up too much! Lightly stir and pour into the Champagne flutes. Decorate with the sprigs of thyme, dashes of orange bitters and serve.

NOTE   If making it for two, use:

◆   a handful of ice
◆   15 parts (150ml/5fl oz) dry sparkling wine
◆   6 parts (40ml/1¾fl oz) gin
◆   2 parts (20ml/4 tsp) lemon juice
◆   2 parts (20ml/4 tsp) lemon & thyme syrup
◆   2 sprigs of thyme

EQUIPMENT

large jug or pitcher
measuring jug

long-handled stirrer
10 Champagne flutes

GINBUCHA

I am a big fan of the effervescent, fermented, tea-based drink kombucha. I think that's because it reminds me of tea and cider, which are two of my favourite drinks. I figured that by adding gin, I could have some fun and turn this gut-healthy drink into a cocktail.

There are a lot of flavoured versions out there, many containing ginger or fruit flavours. Simply adding a gin to these flavoured examples could work nicely – it's just a case of experimenting. This recipe, however, is based on the basic, no-nonsense traditional type of kombucha, the type that is often labelled 'original' and has natural lemony and crisp apple notes. But please note, each producer and each batch will have a slightly different flavour profile and sweetness, so be cautious when adding syrup; start with a teaspoon and add slowly up to 25ml/1fl oz.

PROPORTIONS

1 part gin
4 parts sparkling kombucha
1 part lemon & thyme syrup to taste
   (From a teaspoon up to 1 part – 25ml)

INGREDIENTS

100ml/3½fl oz gin
400ml/14fl oz sparkling kombucha
1 tsp – 25ml/1fl oz lemon & thyme syrup,
   to taste (page 30)
3 handfuls of ice

GARNISH

ice cubes
2 wedges of lemon

1   Pour all the liquid ingredients into a jug along with a handful of ice. Stir gently. Add the ice cubes to the 2 glasses and then pour the cocktail into the glasses.

2   Place the lemon wedges amongst the ice and serve.

EQUIPMENT

jug
measuring jug

stirrer
2 lowball glasses

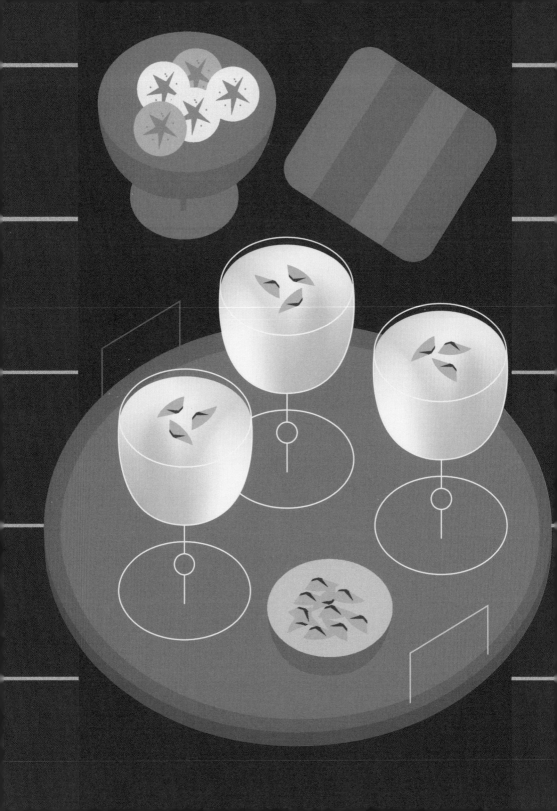

THE VELVET BANANA

Sometimes, the luxurious feeling of sipping a cream liqueur is every bit as satisfying as having an indulgent dessert, and that's exactly the feeling you get when you sip this drink. I'll confess, I'm not the hugest banana fan but for some reason I adore this cocktail.

It's particularly important you use a really good-quality banana liqueur. I used Giffard's Banane du Bresil, which is a Cognac-based liqueur and is absolutely exquisite. Also, being Cognac based, it does not split in cream, unlike rum-based liqueurs.

PROPORTIONS

1 part gin
1 part banana liqueur
1 part single (light) cream

INGREDIENTS

a handful of ice
75ml/2½fl oz gin
75ml/2½fl oz banana liqueur
75ml/2½fl oz single (light) cream

GARNISH

2 dried banana chips for a crumb

1   Crush the banana to make the garnish.

2   Put the ice and all the liquid ingredients into a shaker. Shake for 20 seconds, or until the shaker is cold to the touch, and then strain into the glasses.

3   Garnish with a pinch of crushed dried banana chips over the surface of each cocktail.

EQUIPMENT

cocktail shaker
spice grinder or
  pestle and mortar

strainer
2 dessert
  wine glasses

FIRESIDE FINISHER

After a meal it's always nice to have a digestive to finish the evening. I love nothing better than having a drink in hand whilst sitting in a comfy chair by a roaring fire, and this drink is the perfect winter warmer. Apricot brandy has a wonderfully warming and rounded fruity flavour which comes alive when complemented by good gin and the nutty almond notes of amaretto.

PROPORTIONS

3 parts gin
2 parts amaretto
2 parts apricot brandy
1 part lemon juice

INGREDIENTS

150ml/5fl oz gin
100ml/3½fl oz amaretto
100ml/3½fl oz apricot brandy
50ml/1½fl oz lemon juice
a handful of ice
2 clementine ice cubes (page 39)

GARNISH

2 lemon peel roses (page 35)

1   Put all the liquid ingredients into a jug along with a handful of ice. Stir gently. Add the clementine ice cubes to the 2 glasses and then pour the cocktail into the glasses.

2   Decorate each drink by balancing the lemon peel rose on the rim of the glass.

EQUIPMENT

jug
measuring jug
stirrer

2 cocktail sticks
2 lowball glasses

CANDY CANE DREAM

There's something about chocolate and mint that makes me think of Christmas. Every time I head to New York City on the run up to the big day, I love the cold, the Christmas shop displays, the sparkly lights, the ice skating and the peppermint bark! For those of you that haven't tried peppermint bark, it's basically a broken up slab of white chocolate, dark chocolate and shards of candy cane sweets. Christmas wouldn't be Christmas without a trip to Williams-Sonoma to pick up a tin or two of this delicious confection, and I want to recreate a decadent sipping version that will get you all festive! It's super-easy as it uses pre-made chocolate milkshake that you can buy in shops. Just choose an indulgent one that is going to make you smile. This cocktail is a proper minty nod to the all-American Christmas, but can be enjoyed all year round!

PROPORTIONS

1 part gin
3 parts chocolate milkshake
1 parts crème de menthe

INGREDIENTS

100ml/3½fl oz gin
200ml/7fl oz chocolate milkshake
100ml/3½fl oz crème de menthe
1 egg white
a handful of ice

GARNISH

2 mint candy cane sweets for the candy cane crumb (page 37)

1 Create your candy cane crumb and cover the rim of the glasses with it.

2 Whisk the egg white until foamy and forming peaks.

3 Put all the liquid ingredients into the shaker along with half the whisked egg white and a handful of ice. Shake for 20 seconds more, or until the shaker is cold to the touch. Strain into the glasses.

4 Spoon the other half of the egg white on top of the drinks so that there is a thin white layer on top.

5 Sprinkle the pinch of candy cane crumb over the surface of the drink, add your candy cane stirrers and serve.

NOTE Chocolate milkshakes vary in flavour and viscosity. If the chocolate milkshake you use is a little runny, add a tablespoon or two of double (heavy) cream to make it more luxurious. And if you're a fan of hot chocolate, you could make this using your favourite. All you need to do is make the hot chocolate, let it cool, chill it in the fridge, then use it instead of the milkshake.

EQUIPMENT

cocktail shaker
measuring jug
pestle and mortar
strainer
whisk

2 martini glasses
2 candy cane stirrers (use a sweet or a non- edible stirrer)

COOL AS A CUCUMBER

Cucumber is the most relaxing and refreshing of flavours. It's pure, delicate and, most importantly, it complements the botanicals in many gins beautifully. This cocktail is easy to make and is a great example of how the flavour profile of a cocktail doesn't need to be complex to be satisfying. Here, the restrained beauty of cucumber aligns perfectly with the intense herbaceous nature of fresh basil in a cocktail that celebrates fresh green flavour. Make sure that your gin has grassy notes to it and you will love this little beauty!

PROPORTIONS

1 part gin
3 parts cucumber juice

INGREDIENTS

75ml/2½fl oz gin
a small handful of fresh basil leaves
a handful of ice
225ml/8fl oz cucumber juice
   (from 1 cucumber)
1 tsp simple sugar syrup (page 28) (optional)

GARNISH

2 fresh cucumber wheels – use the same cucumber that you use to make the juice.

1   Cut 2 wheels from the middle of the cucumber and set aside for the garnish.

2   To make the cucumber juice, dice a whole cucumber into 1cm/½in cubes. Put it in a blender and blitz until it is deep green in colour and smooth in texture. (One average-sized cucumber will make around 300ml/10fl oz of purée.) Pass the purée through a fine-mesh strainer into a sterilized container and set aside. It should last in the fridge for a week. Shake the juice well before use.

3   Put the gin into a jug along with the basil. Muddle the basil until you can smell the basil infusing the gin. Add the cucumber juice and the ice and stir.

4   Strain into glasses and serve. Decorate with a wheel of cucumber perched on the rim of the glasses.

NOTE   I don't believe this drink needs added sweetness, but if you want to add to the refreshing and delicate flavour of this drink, add half a teaspoon of simple sugar syrup (page 28) to the jug before stirring. But don't add too much! A teaspoon of syrup could be too much.

EQUIPMENT

blender	sharp knife
chopping board	stirrer
jug	storage container
measuring jug	strainer
muddler	2 Nick & Nora glasses

MAKES	GIN TYPES	FLAVOURS	SEASONS
2 servings	London Dry • spiced • peppercorn • coastal	strong • robust • herbaceous • citrus	all year round

EQUILIBRIUM

You know when you're on holiday and you make a connection with a bartender? I don't know if you're like me, but I love getting to know who is fixing my cocktails. When on holiday in Santorini, we stayed at a gorgeous boutique hotel called Istoria where we met George, the guy in charge of cocktails. We'd get chatting and evening talk turned to his tattoos, particularly the one that said 'equilibrium 00:00'. The story goes that after a turbulent time in his personal life, George realized that he needed to reset his life. He needed to find equilibrium.

Inspired by George's story and his creativity, I've come up with a unique gin cocktail that I hope – if sipped slowly and savoured in small amounts – may help create a sense of balance that can make you feel like the influences in your life have been and are still positive. Keep smiling everyone.

PROPORTIONS

5 parts gin
1 part rosemary & bay syrup
1 part lemon juice

INGREDIENTS

a handful of ice
125ml/4fl oz gin
25ml/1½ tbsp rosemary
  & bay syrup (page 32)
25ml/1½ tbsp lemon juice
2 large ice cubes
a generous dashes of orange bitters
  (around 1 teaspoon)
a generous grind of black pepper

GARNISH

2 sprigs of rosemary
lemon peel ribbons (page 32)

1   Put the handful of ice into a jug and add all the liquid ingredients. Stir gently.

2   Put a large ice cube in each glass and rub your lemon ribbons around the rim of the glasses and surround the ice cubes with the lemon ribbons. Pour in the cocktail, dividing it evenly. Add a sprig of rosemary to each glass and serve.

3   Add more bitters and black pepper to find your equilibrium.

EQUIPMENT

jug
stirrer
2 lowball glasses

ROYAL GIN-GER

The fire in ginger provides a wonderful base for a cocktail, especially a short cocktail. The intensity of flavour when accompanied by a warming gin like an Old Tom can be invigorating. I've always been a fan of The King's Ginger, a liqueur inspired by the original version formulated in 1903 for His Majesty King Edward VII by Berry Bros. & Rudd of London. This cocktail is both refreshing and warming and is certainly fit for parties thrown by a monarch – or even us subjects!

INGREDIENTS

a handful of ice
75ml/2½fl oz gin
75ml/2½fl oz The King's Ginger
25ml/1½ tbsp dry white vermouth
25ml/1½ tbsp lime juice

GARNISH

2 lime peel ringlets (page 35)

PROPORTIONS

3 parts gin
3 parts The King's Ginger
1 part dry white vermouth
1 part lime juice

1   Put the ice and all the liquid ingredients into a shaker. Shake for 20 seconds, or until the shaker is cold to the touch, and then strain into the glasses.

2   Garnish with the lime peel ringlets and serve.

EQUIPMENT

cocktail shaker
strainer
2 Nick & Nora glasses

GIN APPLE TODDY

A hot toddy is both comforting and restorative. Whether you feel you need a hot hug in a mug or if you're feeling under the weather, this cocktail using cloudy apple juice hits the spot. It's also great for outdoor occasions at night like firework displays. I've given this cocktail a hint of toffee apple by using a combination of dark spiced rum and salted caramel liqueur to complement the gin and the cloudy apple juice — it reminds me of enjoying the fun of the fairground at night.

PROPORTIONS

2 parts gin
8 parts cloudy apple juice
1 part dark spiced rum
1 part salted caramel liqueur

INGREDIENTS

100ml/3½fl oz gin
400ml/14fl oz cloudy apple juice
50ml/1½fl oz dark spiced rum
50ml/1½fl oz salted caramel liqueur
1 cinnamon stick
1 star anise
2 cloves

GARNISH

2 fresh apple wheels
sprinkle of salt

1   Put the saucepan on the hob over a gentle heat. Add all the liquid ingredients to the saucepan along with the cinnamon stick, star anise and cloves. Let it gently heat but don't let it boil.

2   Once it starts to bubble, let it simmer gently for 5 minutes. Take it off the heat and let it rest for 5 minutes. Pour into a jug and let it rest for a further 5 minutes.

3   Divide between the heatproof cups and garnish each cup with a wheel of apple on the rim. Add a pinch of salt to the top of each mug.

NOTE   If spiced rum isn't your thing, feel free to try this with bourbon, brandy, whisky or whiskey.

EQUIPMENT

chopping board
hob
jug
measuring jug
saucepan
sharp knife

wooden spoon
2 heatproof cups with handles (glass, brass or copper are great)

LILIBET

When Queen Elizabeth II passed in September 2022, the world lost a great human being. She had been a magnificent and focused ruler for 70 years. Whilst the world went into shock, we realized that the period of mourning should be a celebration of a long and magnificent life. We heard so many stories from those who knew her and we seemed to learn something new about her every day. Queen Elizabeth II's childhood nickname was Lilibet, a name which I think is a beautiful and playful title, one that suits the pictures of her as a young child. The name made me smile and gave me inspiration to create a cocktail in celebration of her unprecedented life. One thing I was aware of was her love of a gin and Dubonnet cocktail. (Dubonnet being a sweet, red aromatized wine-based beverage) so I wanted to use this as a basis of a cocktail I hope would make her smile.

PROPORTIONS

4 parts gin
8 parts Dubonnet
2 parts white vermouth
1 part lemon juice

INGREDIENTS

3 handfuls of ice
100ml/3½fl oz gin
200ml/7fl oz dubonnet
50ml/1½fl oz white vermouth
25ml/1½ tbsp lemon juice

GARNISH

2 lemon peel roses (page 35)

1   Put a handful of ice into the jug and add all the liquid ingredients. Stir gently. Fill your glasses with ice cubes and pour in the cocktail.

2   Decorate each drink by balancing the lemon peel rose on the rim of the glass.

EQUIPMENT

jug
stirrer

2 cocktail sticks
2 small wine glases

DRINKS
FOR EASY
ENTERTAINING

I know that some people are put off the idea of making cocktails for groups of friends or family because they think it's going to take ages — well, that's not always the case! In the time that it takes to fix a cocktail for one or two people, you can fix cocktails for many! And some can be prepared in advance and simply served when guests arrive. Here are a few gin cocktails that are going to make life easy and cocktail parties fun.

PINK GRAPEFRUIT MARTINI

One of the many great things about a Martini is that it is so versatile. The bittersweet notes of pink grapefruit work really well with citrus-forward gins and herbaceous dry vermouth. This pink grapefruit martini uses one of my favourite syrups from this book and is perfect for the start of a dinner or party. And just to show you that it doesn't have to be a drink made in a shaker for two, I've created a batch version (which can easily be scaled down) and you can even make it ahead of time.

PROPORTIONS

2 parts gin
1 part pink grapefruit syrup
1 part lemon juice
1 part dry white vermouth

INGREDIENTS

300ml/10fl oz gin
150 ml/5fl oz pink grapefruit syrup (page 29)
150ml/5fl oz lemon juice
150ml/5fl oz dry white vermouth

GARNISH

6 pink grapefruit crisps (page 37)
pink grapefruit dust (page 37)

1   Make the pink grapefruit syrup, then the crisps and dust. Dust the rims of your glasses. (All of this can be stored and used again for ease – you don't have to do this every time!)

2   Put the ice and all the liquid ingredients into a jug and gently stir until blended and cold. Strain into the glasses, ensuring the ice does not enter the glasses.

3   Decorate with a pink grapefruit crisp in the centre of each glass.

NOTE   If making this ahead of time, simply put the ice and all the liquid ingredients into a jug and gently stir, until blended. Cover the jug and leave in the fridge until ready. When you are ready to serve, add a little ice, stir again and strain into glasses.

EQUIPMENT

large jug or pitcher   strainer
stirrer   6 martini glasses

CRANBERRY COOLER

I know a cooler traditionally means a drink with wine in it, but I couldn't name this drink anything else. It is the perfect refresher for when it feels hotter than the surface of the sun outside! I love the tannic edge that cranberry juice drink gives a cocktail when mixed with the right ingredients. You really get a sense of those red cranberry skins working wonders with the juniper in a top-quality gin. This is a happy cocktail and the gentle pink colour is especially inviting.

PROPORTIONS

4 parts gin
1 part lime juice
1 part orange syrup
4 parts cranberry juice drink
6 parts sparkling water

INGREDIENTS

a handful of ice
300ml/10fl oz gin
75ml/2½fl oz lime juice
75ml/2½fl oz orange syrup (page 30)
300ml/10fl oz cranberry juice drink
450ml/15¾fl oz sparkling water
6 handfuls of cranberry & rosemary
  ice cubes (page 40)

GARNISH

6 dried lime wheels (page 36)

1   Put a handful of ice and all the liquid ingredients, apart from the sparkling water, into the jug. Stir until blended. Gently add the sparkling water and slowly stir again until cold.

2   Put a handful of cranberry and rosemary ice cubes into each glass, strain the drink into the glasses and decorate each glass with a wheel of dried lime on the surface of each drink.

NOTE   For a richer berry flavour use sloe gin, but consider using less syrup.

EQUIPMENT

large jug or pitcher
measuring jug
stirrer

strainer
6 balloon glasses

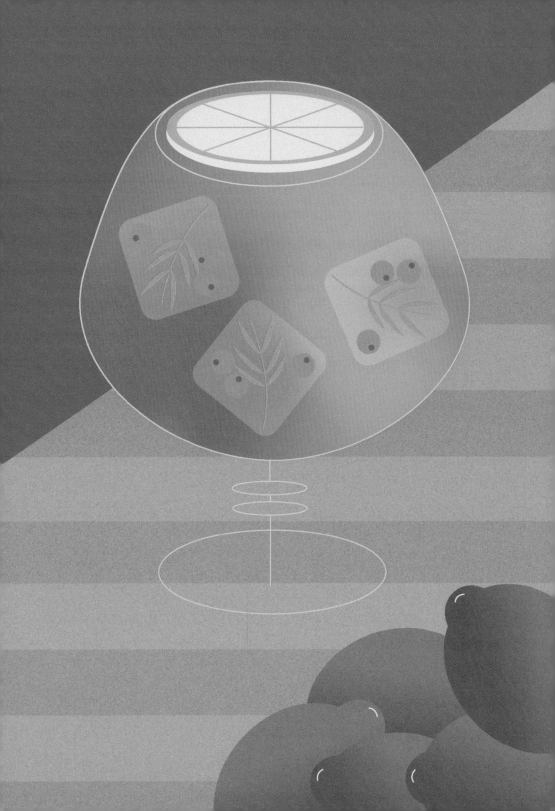

BLOOD ORANGE BOMB

Blood orange is full of flavour and has an unctuous texture that blends beautifully in the right cocktail. It's also easy to find pre-squeezed in supermarkets.

This cocktail is a lovely way to serve liquid sunshine in a pitcher! Great as a daytime treat in the sun as it isn't hugely alcoholic; equally good to put the holiday vibe back into a dark rainy day. It's super-easy to make and your guests will love every sip.

PROPORTIONS

4 parts blood orange juice
3 parts sparkling water
2 parts gin
1 part lime juice

INGREDIENTS

7 handfuls of ice
500ml/17fl oz blood orange juice
375ml/12¾fl oz sparkling water
250ml/8½fl oz gin
125ml/4fl oz lime juice

GARNISH

6 dried blood orange (or normal orange) wheels (page 36)

1   Put a handful of ice and all the liquid ingredients, apart from the sparkling water, into a jug and stir until blended. Gently add the sparkling water and slowly stir again until cold.

2   Put a handful of ice into each glass, strain the drink into the glasses and decorate with a dried orange wheel on the rim of each glass.

EQUIPMENT

large jug or pitcher   strainer
stirrer   6 balloon glasses

GIN RICKY

The gin rickey is a classic gin highball cocktail. Rumour has it that the rickey was invented in the 1880s and was named after Democratic lobbyist Colonel Joe Rickey. Whether he had a hand in its invention or not is unclear, but it was originally made with bourbon, then in the 1890s it became popular when bourbon was replaced by gin.

It is a great gin cocktail to make in a batch because it's so simple to prepare and, let's face it, who doesn't love a long, refreshing, sparkling gin cocktail whether on a hot day or a stormy night? Classically it contains no sweeteners, but if it's a bit too zingy for you (which it was for me), add a little dash of lime and black pepper syrup to reset the flavour balance.

PROPORTIONS

4 parts gin
1 part lime juice
8 parts sparkling water

INGREDIENTS

7 handfuls of ice
400ml/14fl oz gin
100ml/3½fl oz lime juice
800ml/28fl oz sparkling water
1 lime
2 tsp lime & black pepper syrup
  (page 31) (optional)

GARNISH

2 fresh lime wheels
  (additional to the lime above)

1   Put a handful of ice, the gin and lime juice into a jug, and stir until blended. Gently add the sparkling water and slowly stir again until cold. Add the slices of one lime and make sure they are evenly distributed through the ice.

2   Put a handful of ice into each glass, strain the drink into the glasses and decorate each one with a lime wheel on the rim.

3   If required, add a teaspoon of lime & black pepper syrup to each glass (to taste) and stir.

EQUIPMENT

chopping board
large jug or pitcher
measuring jug
sharp knife

stirrer
strainer
6 highball glasses

SANTORINI SUNSET

I love a sunset! Upon our arrival on the beautiful Greek island of Santorini, the first thing we did was grab a cocktail by the pool as the sun set. The colours of the cocktail were so vibrant that I had to try and replicate its visual charm when back home. Even though the ingredients in the cocktail weren't anything like what I have used, it inspired me to come up with the name of this cocktail as a nod to poolside sunsets everywhere.

Serving this drink in collins glasses looks elegant, but if you don't have any, use a highball instead. They give a similar feel.

PROPORTIONS

2 parts gin
3 parts passionfruit puree
3 parts clementine juice
1 part lime juice
2 parts cranberry juice drink (or to taste)

INGREDIENTS

7 handfuls of raspberry
 & mint ice cubes (page 38)
200ml/7fl oz gin
300ml/10fl oz passionfruit purée
300ml/10fl oz clementine juice
100m/3½fl oz lime juice
200ml/7fl oz cranberry juice drink (or to taste)

GARNISH

6 sprigs of mint

1   Put a handful of ice and all the liquid ingredients apart from the cranberry juice drink into a jug and stir until blended and cold.

2   Fill the glasses with the remaining ice and strain the liquid contents of the jug into the glasses. Top each glass with a dash of cranberry juice drink, place a sprig of mint in each drink and your liquid sunset is ready!

NOTE   This is not a strong cocktail. It is more refreshing and fruity than alcoholic. If you fancy more of a kick, up the gin by 1 part (100ml/3½fl oz).

EQUIPMENT

large jug or pitcher
measuring jug
stirrer

strainer
6 collins glasses

MAKES
10 servings

GIN TYPES
London Dry •
citrus • floral

FLAVOURS
citrus • refreshing

SEASONS
spring • summer

FRENCH 75

A cocktail using dry sparkling wine is the perfect batch cocktail, and the French 75 is going to please everybody. The cocktail was originally made at Harry's New York Bar in Paris and supposedly named after a 75-millimetre gun from the World War I era, which was used by French soldiers. Traditionally, it consists of gin, Champagne, lemon juice and simple syrup, but don't feel you have to use Champagne, simply choose your favourite dry sparkling wine and share the love with friends and family.

I based my Garden Party Bubbly on this, so if you fancy a twist on this classic, head to page 86. And if you don't have any sugar syrup to hand, use a sweet sparkling wine like Asti from Northern Italy. Just taste the cocktail as you're adding the gin and lemon juice, then you'll get the sweetness balance just right.

PROPORTIONS

15 parts dry sparkling wine
6 parts gin
4 parts lemon juice
1 part simple sugar syrup

INGREDIENTS

a large handful of ice
750ml/ dry sparkling wine
300ml/10fl oz gin
200ml/7fl oz lemon juice
50ml/1½fl oz simple sugar syrup (page 28)

GARNISH

10 lemon peel ringlets (page 35)

1   Put the ice into the jug. Add the gin, lemon juice and syrup.

2   Open the dry sparkling wine and gently add to the jug, slowly pouring with the jug at an angle so it doesn't froth up too much! Gently stir and strain into the Champagne flutes, ensuring the ice does not enter the glasses.

3   Garnish each glass with a lemon ringlet.

NOTE   Amounts if making it for two:

♦   a handful of ice
♦   150ml/5fl oz dry sparkling wine
♦   60ml/2fl oz gin
♦   40ml/1¾fl oz lemon juice
♦   2 tsp simple sugar syrup
♦   2 lemon peel ringlets

EQUIPMENT

large jug or pitcher
measuring jug
stirrer

strainer
10 Champagne flutes

LATE SUMMER SPRITZ

You may have gathered by now that I love pink grapefruit. The bittersweet citrus notes are beguiling with good gin. Pink grapefruit tonic is a beautiful thing. It marries nicely with gin when there are other ingredients to bridge their flavour profiles. The punch of triple sec and the zing of lime work perfectly here to help bring everything together. Serving this cocktail in a lowball glass is a nice touch because it allows you to use one large ice cube rather than lots of ice. It's the perfect use for the beautiful clementine ice cubes featured on page 39.

PROPORTIONS

2 parts gin
8 parts pink grapefruit soda water
1 part triple sec
1 part lime juice

INGREDIENTS

a handful of ice
200ml/7fl oz gin
800ml/28fl oz pink grapefruit soda water
100ml/3½fl oz triple sec
100ml/3½fl oz lime juice
6 clementine ice cubes (page 39)

GARNISH

6 lime peel ringlets (page 35)

1   Put a handful of ice and all the liquid ingredients, apart from the pink grapefruit soda water, into a jug and stir until blended. Gently add the pink grapefruit soda water, then slowly stir until cold.

2   Put a clementine ice cube into each glass, strain the drink into the glasses and decorate each glass with a lime peel ringlet.

NOTE   If you can't find pink grapefruit soda water, use Indian tonic water and add a dash of pink grapefruit juice and lemon juice for that zesty edge.

EQUIPMENT

large jug or pitcher
measuring jug
stirrer

strainer
6 lowball glasses

SLOE FROSÉ

I first came across the concept of a frosé when I was in Miami a few years ago. Yes, it's basically rosé wine frozen! Ever since I've really enjoyed playing with this concept and making different cocktails using frozen rosé.

I love the way that rosé wine and sloe gin go together. It's a great combination. However, they can vary in fruit profile and sweetness, so a batch of this cocktail for one person may taste different from one made by somebody else. I feel I need to say this before you start making this cocktail – if you're tempted to make it sweeter, you can always add a dash of raspberry syrup (page 33) but I urge you to be cautious – because when the frosé melts it becomes even sweeter as it adjusts to ambient temperature.

PROPORTIONS

5 parts rosé wine
3 parts sloe gin
1 part cranberry juice drink

INGREDIENTS

750ml /2¼fl oz frosé wine
450ml/15¾fl oz sloe gin
150ml/5fl oz cranberry juice drink

GARNISH

a bag of frozen mixed berries
8 sprigs of mint

1   Pour all the liquid ingredients into the freezable container (if you taste it now, it will taste quite sweet and potent, but never fear – the magic is in the freezing!) Clip the container shut and put in the freezer until it has frozen. It is best to leave it overnight or for at least 8 hours.

2   Because of the alcohol, it will not freeze totally solid. Once it has frozen as much as it can, it may appear slightly slushy in places, making it easy to break up.

3   To serve, gently jab the frozen mixture with a butter knife or fork and gently loosen the frozen mixture into icy, slushy shards. Once it has broken up a bit, gently stir with a spoon, then divide among the wine glasses and top with a couple of spoonfuls of frozen mixed berries and a sprig of mint.

EQUIPMENT

freezable container that clips shut
measuring jug
stirrer

knife or fork and spoon
10 large wine glasses

THE MORNING AFTER

I love to encourage people to drink positively. Only fix a drink to make you smile. Drinking gin cocktails should be celebratory. (And always sip a glass of water for every cocktail imbibed!)

But sometimes we overdo it (I know that I can get slightly over-enthusiastic once the drinks are flowing!) and I know from experience that sometimes a little snifter the next morning can actually sort you out! 'Hair of the dog' can be a good thing.

With this in mind, I've come up with some little beauties that might make the morning after feel nearly as good as the night before...

MARMALADE MARTINI

Marmalade is the ultimate breakfast condiment and I love to use it in cooking and cocktail making too. Whatever type of marmalade you go for, be it classic orange, or an alternative like lime, pink grapefruit or mixed citrus, the unique bittersweet zesty flavour of marmalade makes a great martini. The botanical nature of gin is balanced out beautifully by dry white vermouth but is ramped up when citrus zest is added to the equation.

PROPORTIONS

4 parts gin
1 part dry white vermouth
1 part orange marmalade

INGREDIENTS

a handful of ice
150ml/5fl oz gin
50ml/1½fl oz dry white vermouth
2 tsp lemon juice
50ml/1½fl oz orange marmalade
2 strips of lemon peel

GARNISH

2 orange peel ringlets (page 35)

1   Put the ice, all the liquid ingredients and the marmalade (including the shreds of peel) into a shaker. Shake for 20 seconds, or until the shaker is cold to the touch, and then strain into the glasses. I love to make sure that some shreds of citrus peel enter the glass as they look delightful in the drink.

2   Take a small piece of orange peel, twist it over the drink to release the oils, then rub around the rim of the glass. Repeat with a fresh piece for the second glass, then discard the peel.

3   Decorate each glass with an orange peel ringlet and serve.

EQUIPMENT

cocktail shaker
measuring jug
peeler

strainer
2 martini glasses

IT'S IN THE CAN

I love using a retro ingredient in my cookery and cocktail making. Food and drink memories are really exciting, and I love to be reminded of things I used to eat and drink as a kid. I have memories of this syrupy sweet can of fruit cocktail in fruit jelly as a treat at my Nan and Gramp's house.

I got inspired to use this humble can in a gin cocktail recipe after a lunch cooked by my friend, Malaysian chef Ping Coombes. Ping said that in her experience many dim-sum restaurants and high-end South East Asian eateries serve hors d'oeuvres of poached lobster and prawn in a dressing made from canned fruit cocktail mixed with mayonnaise and salad cream. Fruit (not canned) is a staple in many hotels around the world, which got me thinking that using it in a gin cocktail could be a great hangover cure. After all, essentially this drink is a naughty smoothie!

PROPORTIONS

1 part gin
3 parts fruit cocktail
1 tsp lemon juice

INGREDIENTS

3 handfuls of ice
75ml/2½fl oz gin
225ml/7½fl oz fruit cocktail
1 tsp lemon juice

GARNISH

2 sprigs of mint

1 Open the can and put the entire contents (fruit and syrup) into a blender and blitz until smooth. If you are using a stick blender, put the contents of the can into a bowl and blitz until smooth. Either way, the fruit cocktail should be puréed.

2 Put a handful of ice in the shaker and the other handfuls into the glasses. Add all the liquid ingredients to the shaker. Shake for 20 seconds, or until the shaker is cold to the touch, and then strain into the ice-filled glasses.

3 Decorate each glass with a sprig of mint and serve.

EQUIPMENT

blender or stick blender and a bowl
can opener
cocktail shaker

measuring jug
strainer
2 collins glasses

PICK ME UP & SETTLE ME TUMMY

Ginger beer is ridiculously refreshing and is the perfect pick-me-up / stomach settler at any time of day, but particularly in the morning. This is why it makes sense to enjoy a cocktail when you need to shake out the night before.

I didn't realize when I developed it, but there is a cocktail similar to this called the 'suffering bastard', a cocktail that was designed as a hangover cure for World War II troops at Cairo's Shepheard's Hotel in the 1940s. It is thought that over time both bourbon and brandy have been used in this cocktail but I've opted for Cognac for that touch of velvety French sophistication. But if you have a preference, use whichever dark spirit takes your fancy. You could even use whisky or whiskey.

PROPORTIONS

2 parts gin
2 parts Cognac
1 part lime juice
6 parts ginger beer

INGREDIENTS

50ml/1½fl oz gin
50ml/1½fl oz Cognac
25ml/1½ tbsp lime juice
150ml/5fl oz ginger beer
3 handfuls of ice

GARNISH

2 lime wedges

1   Pour all the liquid ingredients into a jug along with a handful of ice. Stir gently. Add the remaining ice cubes to the glasses and pour the cocktail into the glasses.

2   Decorate each drink with a wedge of lime and serve.

EQUIPMENT

jug
measuring jug

stirrer
2 lowball glasses

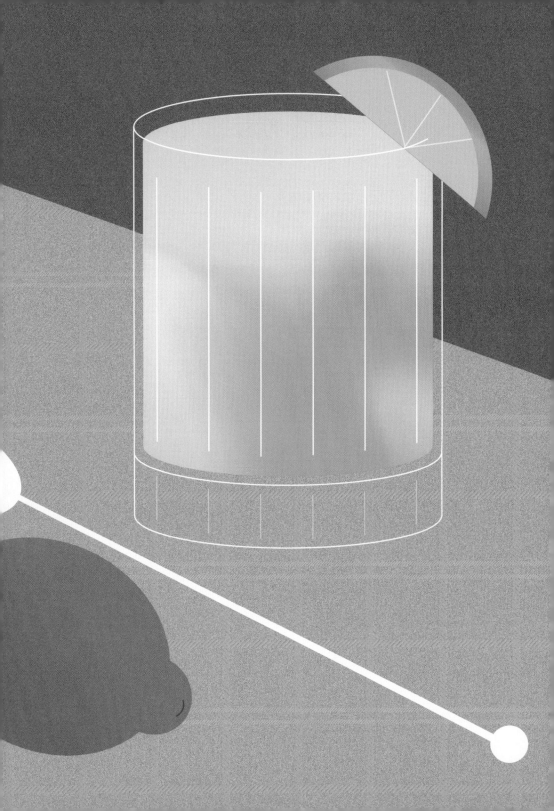

CALIFORNIA GIRL

The title of this cocktail is inspired by a lyric from Katy Perry's 'California Gurls'. She mentions sipping 'gin and juice' and always makes me think of the retro way of drinking gin with orange juice, but I felt I couldn't just give you a recipe for a gin and OJ! So, I imagined, f we'd partied hard until the morning light in Santa Monica, what would be an easy drink to fix on the beach at sunrise?

My hubby loves a can of fizzy orange (when back in Ireland he's partial to a Club Orange) but wherever you are, a canned sparkling orange drink is relatively easy to pick up, so I thought why not combine that with enough gin to awaken you and a dash of one of California's finest exports – peaches! I'm using peach purée made by Funkin because they make the best easy-to-buy and easy-to-use, pre-made cocktail accompaniments.

PROPORTIONS

4 parts gin
6 parts fizzy orange
6 parts sparkling water
2 parts peach purée
1 part lemon juice

INGREDIENTS

100ml/3½fl oz gin
150ml/5fl oz fizzy orange
150ml/5fl oz sparkling water
50ml/1½fl oz peach purée
25ml/1½ tbsp lemon juice
3 handfuls of ice

GARNISH

2 dried orange wheels (page 36)

1   Pour all the liquid ingredients into a jug and add a handful of ice. Stir gently.

2   Add the remaining ice cubes to the glasses and pour the cocktail into the glasses. Decorate each drink with a dried orange wheel on the rim of the glass and serve.

EQUIPMENT

jug
measuring jug

stirrer
2 hurricane glasses

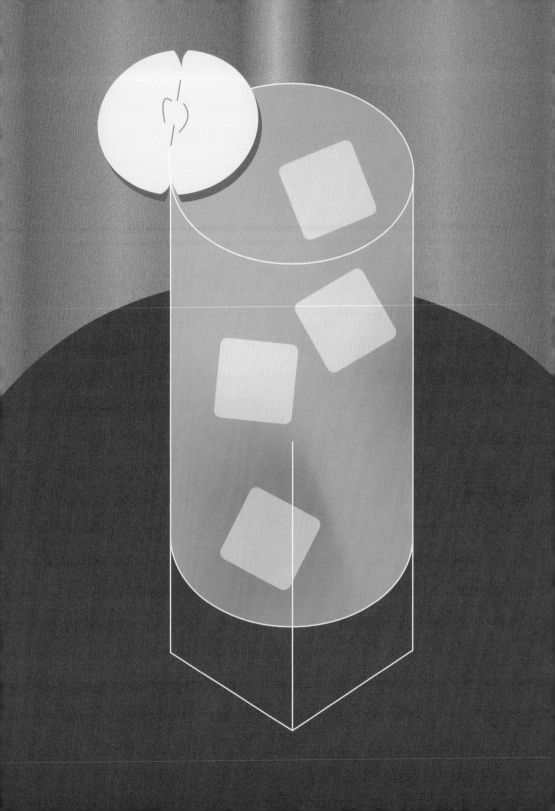

FORBIDDEN APPLE

Whether I pick them fresh off my parent's apple tree, sip their juice in a crisp, cold cider, or enjoy them in a restorative shot of live apple cider vinegar, I love apples! And they're a great breakfast fruit ... so why not put them in a cocktail?

The flavour of a dry (not sweet) cloudy apple juice is a great cocktail ingredient. It brings out both the richer fruit elements in gin as well as the peppery notes in some. This long, cool drink is a great way to disperse the groggy head from the night before with its rich orchard charms and the kick of the appley vinegar.

PROPORTIONS

3 parts gin
1 part apple cider vinegar
6 parts dry cloudy apple juice
8 parts sparkling water

INGREDIENTS

75ml/2½fl oz gin
25ml/1½ tbsp apple cider vinegar
150ml/5fl oz dry cloudy apple juice
3 handfuls of ice cubes
200ml/7fl oz sparkling water

GARNISH

2 apple wheels

1   Pour the gin, cider vinegar and apple juice into the jug along with a handful of ice cubes. Stir gently. Add the sparkling water and gently stir again.

2   Put 2 handfuls of ice cubes in the glasses, then pour the cocktail into the glasses.

3   Decorate each drink with an apple wheel on the rim.

EQUIPMENT

jug
measuring jug

stirrer
2 highball glasses

RESTORATION

For every ruin, there is the chance to be restored. Chilli with fruit does this for me. There's something about that hot and refreshing combo that seems to awaken the senses after a night of overdoing it. I wonder if the thought of lots of vitamin C might also make the restorative nature of this drink alluring. Either way, this cocktail is delicious, has more fruit in it than a breakfast platter and is like a tropical holiday in a glass accompanied by a vigorous shakeout. What more could you want? Cheers everyone!

PROPORTIONS

4 parts gin
2 parts passionfruit purée
3 parts clementine juice

INGREDIENTS

½ red chilli
a handful of basil leaves
100ml/3½fl oz gin
3 handfuls of ice
50ml/1½fl oz passionfruit purée
75ml/2½fl oz clementine juice
1 lime

GARNISH

1 passionfruit
2 small sprigs of basil

1   To make the garnish, cut the passionfruit in half and then take 2 end sprigs of basil and rest each one on top of the passionfruit. Set aside.

2   Chop the chilli into thin slices and put it in the shaker along with the remaining basil and the gin. Muddle the basil leaves and the chilli with the gin. Once you can smell the basil and chilli infusing the gin, add a handful of ice and the other liquid ingredients.

3   Put 2 handfuls of ice in the glasses, shake the shaker for 20 seconds, or until the shaker is cold to the touch, and then strain into the glasses.

4   Float a passionfruit and basil garnish on top of each drink like a boat, or nestle them amongst the ice if the ice is peaking above the surface of the cocktail. Serve immediately.

EQUIPMENT

chopping board
cocktail shaker
measuring jug

muddler
sharp knife
2 lowball glasses

ABOUT THE AUTHOR

The guy with the inquisitive palate, Andy Clarke is one of the 21st century's most exciting voices in the world of food and drink.

Andy was born and raised in the West Country of England, near the vibrant city of Bristol by food-loving parents who were passionate about fruit and veg growing and delicious home cooking. Andy credits them with instilling their passion for food and drink in him at an early age, something he took with him went he went on to study and work in and around the London area as an adult.

Now, happy to call himself a 'professional eater and drinker' Andy has travelled across the world working as a food, drink and travel television producer and director. It was whilst working in television that he started to use his energetic writing style and lively personality to communicate his life-long love of bringing people together through food and drink via his writing and event hosting.

Andy's food and drink recommendations have gained attention across the globe and Andy is very much at his absolute happiest when conveying the merits of all things sippable and edible. He loves nothing better than sharing the love of food and drink on television, through social media, in print and online, and by hosting festivals and events.

Throughout his career, Andy has worked with some of the world's greatest chefs and drinks experts, he is a consultant to the hospitality industry and he regularly judges for international food and drink awards.

Never too far away from his cobbler shakers, Andy now spends a great deal of his time designing cocktails for fun, for live and multimedia events and for brands across the hospitality industry.

Follow him across on social media @tvsandyclarke.

ACKNOWLEDGEMENTS

There are a number of people I can't wait to thank for supporting me through my gin-obsessed journey through adulthood: All the friends and family who have put up with my apothecary as well as the fabulous people who watch me enthuse about food and drink on telly, at festivals and online.

I'd like to give special thanks (drink in hand) to anybody in the drinks, television and publishing industries who has encouraged my do go forward in a world I love. I appreciate it more than you will know. And to anybody who has bought a book that I've written, read one of my articles or tried one of my cocktail recipes – you have given me strength to believe in myself. For this, I am eternally grateful.

The drinks-makers who have furnished me with so many of their great products and fuelled my overactive gin-cocktail-based enthusiasm. Particularly Funkin for their pure pour juice pouches, Giffard for their liqueurs, Ocean Spray for their cranberry juice drinks, and to all the wonderful gin distilleries and drinks producers for the variety of drinks I've tasted along the way. (And a big hug goes to the team at one of my fave restaurants littlefrench in Bristol for rescuing me when – in the middle of recipe testing – I realized I'd run out of green chartreuse!)

Cheers to Scott & Oscar AKA The Ginfluencers UK along with Craig from Mothers Ruin 1751 and Camera Ryan for the hilarious gin cocktail filming we did in the North London Gin Palace before the idea of this book was even conceived. It was certainly a catalyst that got me hungry for more gin ideas. So, let's get those cameras rolling again soon.

Thanks to my friends Nicola Lampkin at Otterbeck Distillery, Katie Overton-Hart at G&H Spirits and Ian Curtis at Madame Jennifer Distillery for answering my geeky gin-based questions and for their guidance. And hugest thanks to Harry Craddock and *The Savoy Cocktail Book* for the hours of tantalising reading and inspiration.

My publisher Kate Pollard deserves a medal (and a stiff gin cocktail) for putting up with me and my over enthusiastic ideas, as does my editor Wendy Hobson. The hugest of thanks go to my fabulous illustrators at Evi-O. Studio for interpreting my ideas into gorgeous images and to the lovely team at Hardie Grant for their professional guidance.

But most of all I want to thank my long-suffering Guinea pig, I mean husband Alan O'Shea for being my first port of call when I have a new idea. (Also, apologies to our neighbours for knocking on their doors at all hours asking their opinion!) I also would like to thank my wonderful family, particularly my mum, Pauline, and my dad, George, for encouraging me to be who I am.

This book is for all of you. Now, stop reading and start cocktailing. Sip happy, you lovely lot!

ALL MY LOVE,
ANDY

INDEX

A

absinthe
Corpse Reviver No. 2 58
amaretto
Fireside Finisher 92
apple cider vinegar
Forbidden Apple 135
apple juice
Forbidden Apple 135
Gin Apple Toddy 102
apple wheels
Forbidden Apple 135
Gin Apple Toddy 102
apricot brandy
Charlie Chaplin 60
Fireside Finisher 92
aquafaba 20
artisan gin 10
Aviation 68

B

balloon glasses 25
banana chips
The Velvet Banana 91
banana liqueur
The Velvet Banana 91
barrel-aged gin 12
basil leaves
Cool as a Cucumber 97
Restoration 136
bay leaves
rosemary & bay syrup 32
Bee's Knees 64
The Bee's Mead 84
Benedictine
Singapore Sling 52
berries, mixed
Sloe Frosé 122
bitters
Equilibrium 98
Garden Party Bubbly 86
Raspberry Gin Sour 80
Singapore Sling 52
blackberries
Bramble 57
Blood Orange Bomb 112
Boston shakers 22
botanicals 13
boutique gin 10

Bramble 57
brandy
Loud Speaker 71
Pick Me Up & Settle
     Me Tummy 130

C

California Girl 132
Campari
Negroni 46
Candy Cane Dream 94
caramel liqueur
Gin Apple Toddy 102
chamomile tea
G & Tea Martini 76
Charlie Chaplin 60
chartreuse, green
Last Word 72
cherry brandy
Singapore Sling 52
chilli
Restoration 136
chocolate milkshake
Candy Cane Dream 94
cinnamon stick
Gin Apple Toddy 102
citrus fruit
oven-dried citrus peel crisps 37
oven-dried fruit wheels 36
the ringlet 35
the rose & the ribbon 35
citrus gins 13
Classic Dry Gin Martini 44
clementine ice cubes 39
Fireside Finisher 92
Late Summer Spritz 120
Negroni 46
clementine juice
Restoration 136
Santorini Sunset 117
Clover Club 54
cloves
Gin Apple Toddy 102
coastal gins 13
cobbler shakers 22
cocktails
equipment 22–4
ingredients 19, 22
tips 19–20
Cognac
Loud Speaker 71
Pick Me Up & Settle
     Me Tummy 130
Cointreau
Loud Speaker 71
cola 17

collins glasses 25
Cool as a Cucumber 97
Corpse Reviver No. 2 58
coupe glasses 25
craft gin 10
cranberry & rosemary
     ice cubes 40
Cranberry Cooler 110
cranberry juice drink
Cranberry Cooler 110
Santorini Sunset 117
Sloe Frosé 122
cream
The Velvet Banana 91
crème de menthe
Candy Cane Dream 94
crème de mûre
Bramble 57
crème de violette
Aviation 68
cucumber juice
Cool as a Cucumber 97
cucumber slices
Cool as a Cucumber 97
cucumber tonic water 17
Victory Spritz 79

D

damson gin 15
dry sparkling wine
French 75 119
Garden Party Bubbly 86
Sparkling Tea 18
dubonnet
Lilibet 105

E

egg white 20
Candy Cane Dream 94
Clover Club 54
Gin Fizz 48
The Grand Lady In a Sidecar 82
Raspberry Gin Sour 80
Equilibrium 98

F

Fireside Finisher 92
flavoured gins 14
floral gins 13
flowers, edible
Aviation 68
Singapore Sling 52
flute glasses 25

Forbidden Apple 135
French 75: 119
fruit
oven-dried fruit wheels 36
fruit cocktail
It's In The Can 128
fruit flavoured gins 14
fruit juice 18

G

G & Tea Martini 76
Garden Party Bubbly 86
garnishes. see also ice cubes
dust or crumb 37
fruit 34
oven-dried citrus peel crisps 37
oven-dried fruit wheels 36
the ringlet 35
the rose & the ribbon 35
Genever 11
Gimlet 63
gin 8–9, 10–15
Aviation 68
Bee's Knees 64
The Bee's Mead 84
Blood Orange Bomb 112
Bramble 57
California Girl 132
Candy Cane Dream 94
Classic Dry Gin Martini 44
Clover Club 54
Cool as a Cucumber 97
Corpse Reviver No. 2 58
Cranberry Cooler 110
Equilibrium 98
Fireside Finisher 92
Forbidden Apple 135
French 75: 119
G & Tea Martini 76
Garden Party Bubbly 86
Gimlet 63
Gin Apple Toddy 102
Gin Fizz 48
Ginbucha 88
The Grand Lady
In a Sidecar 82
It's In The Can 128
Last Word 72
Late Summer Spritz 120
Lilibet 105
Loud Speaker 71
Marmalade Martini 127
Negroni 46
Pick Me Up & Settle
    Me Tummy 130
Pink Grapefruit Martini 108

Raspberry Gin Sour 80
Restoration 136
Royal Gin-Ger 100
Santorini Sunset 117
Singapore Sling 52
Southside 66
Tom Collins 51
The Velvet Banana 91
Victory Spritz 79
Gin Apple Toddy 102
Gin Fizz 48
gin liqueurs 15
Gin Ricky 114
Ginbucha 88
ginger ale 17
ginger beer 17
Pick Me Up & Settle
    Me Tummy 130
glassware 25–7
The Grand Lady
    In a Sidecar 82
Grand Marnier
The Grand Lady In a Sidecar 82

H

highball glasses 27
history of gin 6–7
honey syrup 29
Bee's Knees 64
G & Tea Martini 76
honeycomb
The Bee's Mead 84
hurricane glasses 27

I

ice/ice cubes 20
clementine ice cubes 39
cranberry & rosemary
ice cubes 40
lemon & thyme ice cubes 39
raspberry & mint ice cubes 38
ingredients 19, 22
It's In The Can 128

J

jiggers 22
jugs 23
juicers 23
juniper berries 6

K

The King's Ginger

Royal Gin-Ger 100
kombucha 18
Ginbucha 88

L

Last Word 72
Late Summer Spritz 120
lemon & thyme syrup 30–1
Garden Party Bubbly 86
Ginbucha 88
lemon juice
Aviation 68
Bee's Knees 64
The Bee's Mead 84
Bramble 57
California Girl 132
Clover Club 54
Corpse Reviver No. 2 58
Equilibrium 98
Fireside Finisher 92
French 75: 119
Garden Party Bubbly 86
Gin Fizz 48
The Grand Lady In a Sidecar 82
It's In The Can 128
Lilibet 105
Loud Speaker 71
Marmalade Martini 127
Pink Grapefruit Martini 108
Tom Collins 51
Victory Spritz 79
lemon peel
Classic Dry Gin Martini 44
Corpse Reviver No. 2 58
Equilibrium 98
Fireside Finisher 92
French 75: 119
G & Tea Martini 76
Lilibet 105
Marmalade Martini 127
Tom Collins 51
lemon wedges
Ginbucha 88
lemons
Gin Fizz 48
lemon & thyme ice cubes 39
lemon & thyme syrup 30–1
Lilibet 105
lime & black pepper syrup 31
Gin Ricky 114
lime juice
Blood Orange Bomb 112
Charlie Chaplin 60
Cranberry Cooler 110
Gimlet 63
Gin Ricky 114

Last Word 72
Late Summer Spritz 120
Pick Me Up & Settle
  Me Tummy 130
Raspberry Gin Sour 80
Royal Gin-Ger 100
Santorini Sunset 117
Singapore Sling 52
Southside 66
lime peel
Late Summer Spritz 120
lime wedges
Pick Me Up & Settle
  Me Tummy 130
lime wheels
Cranberry Cooler 110
Gimlet 63
Gin Ricky 114
Southside 66
limes
lime & black pepper syrup 31
London Dry 10
Loud Speaker 71
low alcohol gins 20
lowball glasses 27

M

manufacturing gin 8–9
maraschino liqueur
Aviation 68
Last Word 72
Marmalade Martini 127
Martini
Classic Dry Gin Martini 44
G & Tea Martini 76
Pink Grapefruit Martini 108
martini glasses 27
mead
The Bee's Mead 84
measuring ingredients 19, 22
mint
It's In The Can 128
raspberry & mint ice cubes 38
Raspberry Gin Sour 80
Santorini Sunset 117
Sloe Frosé 122
Southside 66
Victory Spritz 79
mixers 16–18
muddlers/muddling 20, 24
mugs 27

N

Navy Strength 11
Negroni 46
New Western Dry Gin 10
Nick & Nora glasses 27
non-alcoholic gins 20

O

old-fashioned glasses 27
Old Tom 11
orange juice
Blood Orange Bomb 112
California Girl 132
orange peel
Charlie Chaplin 60
The Grand Lady In a Sidecar 82
Loud Speaker 71
Negroni 46
orange syrup 30
Cranberry Cooler 110
orange wheels
Blood Orange Bomb 112
oranges
orange syrup 30

P

passion fruit
Restoration 136
passion fruit purée
Restoration 136
Santorini Sunset 117
peach purée
California Girl 132
pepper
Equilibrium 98
lime & black pepper syrup 31
pestle & mortar 24
**Pick Me Up & Settle
  Me Tummy 130**
pineapple juice
Singapore Sling 52
pink gin 12
Pink Grapefruit Martini 108
pink grapefruit soda 17
Late Summer Spritz 120
pink grapefruit syrup 29
Pink Grapefruit Martini 108
pitchers 23
Plymouth Gin 11

Q

quinine 16

R

raspberries
Clover Club 54
raspberry & mint ice cubes 38
Raspberry Gin Sour 80
raspberry syrup 33
Victory Spritz 79
raspberry & mint ice cubes 38
Santorini Sunset 117
Raspberry Gin Sour 80
raspberry syrup 33
Clover Club 54
Raspberry Gin Sour 80
Victory Spritz 79
Restoration 136
rocks glasses 27
rosé wine
Sloe Frosé 122
rosemary
cranberry & rosemary
  ice cubes 40
Equilibrium 98
Last Word 72
rosemary & bay syrup 32
rosemary & bay syrup 32
Equilibrium 98
Royal Gin-Ger 100
rum
Gin Apple Toddy 102

S

Santorini Sunset 117
shakers/shaking 20, 22
sherbet lemon
Bee's Knees 64
Victory Spritz 79
shrubs 33
simple sugar syrup 28
Bramble 57
Cool as a Cucumber 97
French 75: 119
Gimlet 63
Gin Fizz 48
Southside 66
Tom Collins 51
Sloe Frosé 122
sloe gin 15
Charlie Chaplin 60
Sloe Frosé 122
smoked gin 12
sodas 17

Southside 66
sparkling tea 18
sparkling water
Blood Orange Bomb 112
California Girl 132
Cranberry Cooler 110
Forbidden Apple 135
Gin Fizz 48
Gin Ricky 114
Tom Collins 51
spiced gins 13
star anise
Gin Apple Toddy 102
stemmed wine glasses 27
sterilizing 24
stirring/stirrers 24
strainers 24
sugar 29
lemon & thyme syrup 30–1
lime & black pepper syrup 31
orange syrup 30
raspberry syrup 33
rosemary & bay syrup 32
simple sugar syrup 28
syrups
honey syrup 29
lemon & thyme syrup 30–1
lime & black pepper syrup 31
orange syrup 30
pink grapefruit syrup 29
raspberry syrup 33
rosemary & bay syrup 32
simple sugar syrup 28

T
tea 18
G & Tea Martini 76
thyme
Garden Party Bubbly 86
lemon & thyme ice cubes 39
lemon & thyme syrup 30–1
Tom Collins 51
tonic water 16
triple sec
Corpse Reviver No. 2 58
Late Summer Spritz 120
Loud Speaker 71

V
The Velvet Banana 91
vermouth
Classic Dry Gin Martini 44
Corpse Reviver No. 2 58
G & Tea Martini 76
Lilibet 105
Marmalade Martini 127
Negroni 46
Pink Grapefruit Martini 108
Royal Gin-Ger 100
Victory Spritz 79

W
wine
French 75: 119
Garden Party Bubbly 86
wine glasses 27

Z
zest gins 13

Published in 2024 by Hardie Grant Books,
an imprint of Hardie Grant Publishing

Hardie Grant Books (London)
5th & 6th Floors
52–54 Southwark Street
London SE1 1UN

Hardie Grant Books (Melbourne)
Building 1, 658 Church Street
Richmond, Victoria 3121

hardiegrantbooks.com

British Library Cataloguing-in-Publication Data.
A catalogue record for this book
is available from the British Library.

The House of Gin

ISBN: 978-178488-952-4

10 9 8 7 6 5 4 3 2 1

Publishing Director: Kate Pollard

Copy Editor: Wendy Hobson

Proofreader: Kate Wanwimolruk

Design: Evi-O.Studio | Katherine Zhang
Illustration: Evi-O.Studio | Katherine Zhang,
Doreen Zheng

Indexer: Cathy Heath

Production Controller: Martina Georgieva

Colour reproduction by p2d

Printed and bound in China
by Leo Paper Products Ltd.